A PLACE
AT THE LAKE

A PLACE AT THE LAKE

Paul Clifford Larson

AFTON HISTORICAL SOCIETY PRESS

AFTON, MINNESOTA

To Griffin, who already knows the difference

between fishing and catching fish

Library of Congress Cataloging-in-Publication Data
Larson, Paul Clifford.
    A place at the lake / Paul Clifford Larson. — 1st ed.
        p.   cm.
    Includes bibliographical references and index.
    ISBN 1-890434-05-1 (hard cover)
    1. Vacation homes—Minnesota.   2. Cottages—Minnesota.
    3. Lakeside architecture—Minnesota.   4. Minnesota—Social
life and customs.   I. Title.
F607.L35   1998
977.6—dc21   97-53072
                                                                                        CIP

Printed in Canada

Half title page photo: An outing at White Bear Lake in 1891
Frontispiece photo: Emile and Marie Amblard, Mrs. Amblard's mother, their daughter,
and the gardener at the Amblard summer estate on Coney Island, Waconia, ca. 1898

The Afton Historical Society Press is a non-profit organization that takes
pride and pleasure in publishing fine books on Minnesota subjects.

W. Duncan MacMillan, president
Patricia Condon Johnston, publisher

Afton Historical Society Press
P.O. Box 100
Afton, MN 55001
1-800-436-8443

CONTENTS

PREFACE

*Lakes add an indescribable charm and pictorial
beauty to the landscape. They have made
Switzerland the home of the tourist, and the lochs
of Scotland the synonym of romance. In time the
lakes of Minnesota will do all this for us.*

JOHN W. BOND
Minnesota and Its Resources, 1878

IF THE PHRASE "up to the lake" was not born
in Minnesota, it must have arrived on the
first steamer. Minnesotans have carried on a
romance with their lakes for more than a century, and the affair shows no signs of abating.

Artists and photographers have enthusias-
tically recorded favorite Minnesota summering spots since the first wave of Southerners
swarmed north to St. Anthony Falls in the
1850s. I first envisioned the present work as
an ordered collage of these pictures, letting
them do most of the talking and providing
only enough text to breathe life and historical movement into what would otherwise be
a miscellany of static images. And I hope
that the result can still be viewed and appre-
ciated at this fundamental level—an engag-
ing picture book, plain and simple.

But interpreting the images also beckons
us beyond them. Lake cabins may offer
refuge from the tensions of urban life, but
they provide no escape from history. The
railroad and the automobile that impelled
Minnesotans out into the plains and forests
also opened the way to the lakes. Architectural currents that gave order to urban
experience rippled into vacation haunts far
removed from the city. Even changing family
structures and gender roles carried from
principal residence to summer retreat, influ-
encing everything from lot location and
cottage type to daily schedules. Finally, the
chosen environments and habits of vacationing Minnesotans stir age-old conflicts
between farmers and sportsmen, land developers and lovers of wilderness, those who
live for social interaction and those who
guard their privacy. These conflicts make
news in the cities but play themselves out
on still-tranquil settings miles removed from
the forums of law and public opinion.

I have tried to give each of these stories
their due, using the westward and northward expansion of the transportation net-

work as an organizing principle of the
book as a whole. But the focus of the book
throughout remains the lakeside cottages
themselves, with an emphasis on private
homes rather than hotels. Some of the storied
lake resorts of the past have unavoidably
crept into the account, however, for they
were instrumental in opening a lake or lake
region to private summer occupancy, and
more than once served as models for the
humbler structures that grew up at their foot.

Even within these strictures, I have had to
set chronological limits, lest a volume meant
to be a friendly living room or bedside companion grow into a monster shunned by publisher and reader alike. As the account shifts
from scene to scene, the curtain drops as
soon as summer cottagers begin to feel the
elbows of year-round occupants. Minnetonka's story, for example, is followed in
sequence around the lake; but once com-
muters begin to settle in, the tale rushes to a
close, in spite of continued cottage building
at more remote sites along the shore. This
limit allows the geographical arrangement of
the text to approximate a chronological order,

beginning with the garland of lakes around the Twin Cities and culminating in the persisting wilderness of the Arrowhead region.

Most of the images are taken from the collections of Minnesota Historical Society. I am indebted to the research library staff, photographic lab, and historic preservation office for making them available to me. Thomas O'Sullivan was also kind enough to let me sort through Edwin Whitefield's captivating watercolor sketches of Minnesota lakes and to alert me to Minnesota's place on the fashionable tour of pre-Civil War years.

I am also grateful for information and images provided by Jodi Maki of Itasca County Historical Society, Fred Livesay of Carver County Historical Society, Barbara Grover of Douglas County Historical Society, Maureen Galvin of Wright County Historical Society, Barbara Bezat of Northwest Architectural Archives, several staff members of Minneapolis Public Library and St. Paul Public Library, and staff and volunteers at Hennepin County Historical Society, West Hennepin County Pioneers Association, Excelsior-Minnetonka Historical Society, and

Wayzata Public Library. Ann Luther, Jane Bonne, and Jan Forsberg all provided valuable leads regarding White Bear Lake summer cottages. I am also grateful to John Swift of Pike Bay Lodge (the A. B. Coates summer estate), Allen Latham of Medayto, Stuart MacDonald of MacDonald and Mack Architects, and Marjorie Wilson Richison of the Pelican Lake Outing Club for information and pictures about buildings with which they were particularly familiar.

I owe a special debt of gratitude to Mary Graves, historian of Voyageurs National Park, for pictures of surviving private summer cottages within the park boundaries, as well as a wealth of information about the development of the Arrowhead region. Hopefully, the comprehensive documentation she is assembling can soon find public expression beyond the meager examples I was able to include here.

As publisher, Patricia Johnston offers her writers an unusual degree of support, and her comments saved the text from many an obscure remark as well as a few snore-inducing digressions. This is my third book to pass beneath Sally Rubinstein's watchful eye, and the fact that the first draft continues to come back as full of marks as ever testifies both to my slowness as a learner and her continued astuteness as an editor. She leaves my stylistic eccentricities alone, however, for which I may be more grateful than my readers.

To my wife Pam and son Griffin, both Illinois-born, I express the deepest thanks for rekindling my excitement and pleasure in the surpassing beauty of those myriad Minnesota lakes that still beckon us to the deep simplicity of a life in nature.

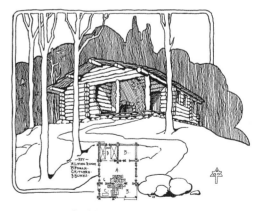

Louis F. Bersbach's second-prize design for the Western Architect Log Cabin Competition *in 1914*

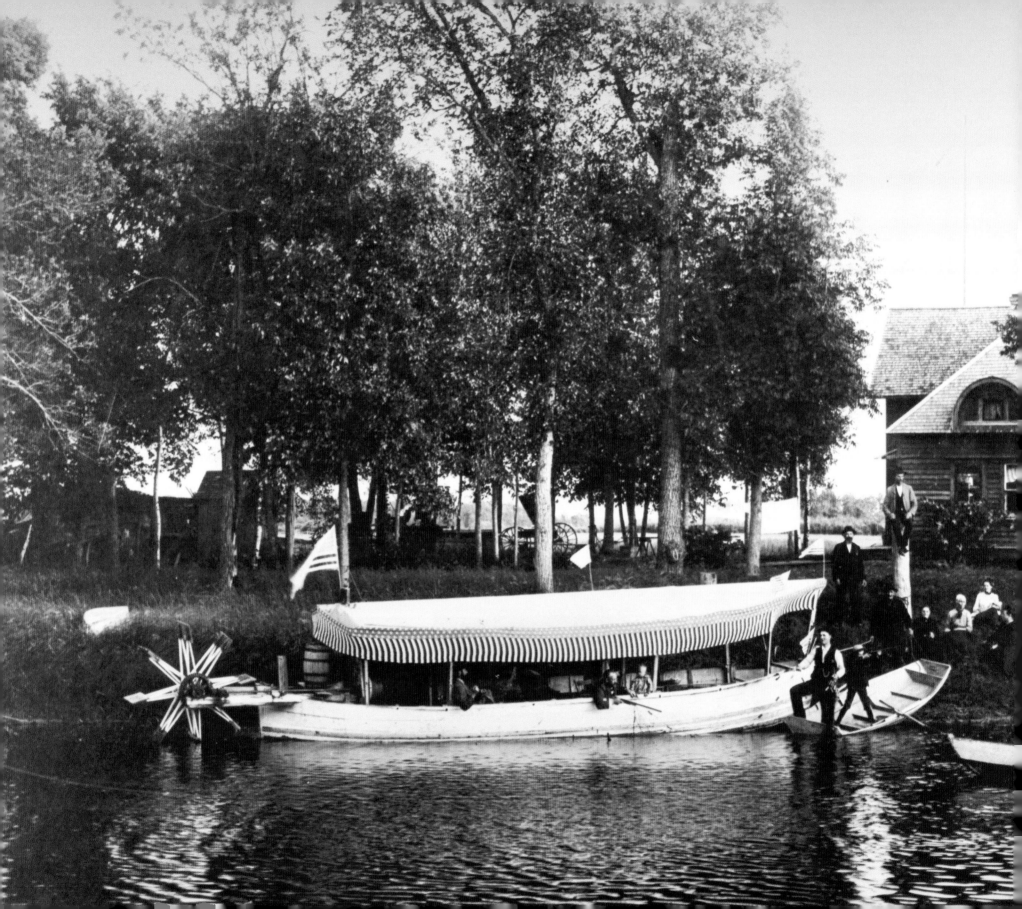

$\mathscr{S}$ARATOGA OF THE WEST

Flying by islands, prairies, woodlands, bluffs is an exhilarating luxury, compared with which all the fashion and tinsel and parade of your Newports and Saratogas are utterly insipid.

JAMES M. GOODHUE, *Minnesota Pioneer*, 1852

MINNESOTA'S LAKES have enticed a stream of tourists and temporary residents for well over a hundred summers. To a modern Midwesterner, spoiled by a road system that can take him to the water's edge, a weekend by the lake has come to seem as natural as a day at the office. But a century and a half ago, when Minnesota stood at the northwestern frontier of the nation, paradise had other guises and the lakes quite a different significance.

Geologist and explorer Henry Schoolcraft, popularly credited with the discovery of the source of the Mississippi River, was the first to hazard a guess at the number of Minnesota's lakes. His astonishing estimate, first ventured in 1851, was immortalized in

House and boats on the Roseau River, ca. 1895

the slogan "Land of Ten Thousand Lakes." That mystifyingly large number helped put the state-to-be on the map. Getting New Englanders to rise from their armchair astonishment or forego the pampering pleasures of the eastern resorts and actually visit one or two of the ten thousand proved to be a far tougher task.[1]

Two lures were dangled before the intrigued but reticent reading public of the East and the South. The first was simply the wilderness itself. As early as 1835, painter George Catlin recommended a "Fashionable Tour" of the Upper Mississippi River that would culminate at St. Anthony Falls. Through the 1840s and 1850s, an increasing number of sightseers took Catlin's advice. Wealthy southerners and easterners set aside their usual comforts and conveniences for the opportunity of experiencing at first-hand the wild scenery of the river above St. Louis before civilization had made its mark.[2]

The birth of journalism in Minnesota Territory added multiple voices to Catlin's. As Theodore Blegen put it, "every newspaper was a tourist bureau." Leading the way

was James M. Goodhue, editor of the *Minnesota Pioneer*. He made his strongest appeal to residents of states and territories bordering on the Mississippi River itself. Epidemics of malaria and cholera were already driving those who could afford it to more northerly climes for the summer. Goodhue invited them to "hurry along through the valley of the Mississippi, its shores studded with town, and farms, flying by islands, prairies, woodlands, bluffs—an ever varied scene of beauty, away up into the land of the wild Dakota, and of cascades and pine forests, and cooling breezes."[3]

Among the first of Minnesota's eastern visitors to leave the steamboat behind and appreciate those far-flung lakes first hand was itinerant artist Edwin Whitefield. Equal parts aesthete, adventurer, and entrepreneur, Whitefield spent his early career, from 1837 to 1856, recording the landscapes and residences of the Hudson and Mississippi Rivers and eastern Canada. In 1856 he traveled up the Mississippi to St. Paul, where he immediately plunged into land speculation and settlement schemes for Minnesota Territory.

His first venture took him due west of St. Paul and Minneapolis, past Lake Minnetonka and along the southern border of what would become known as the state's Lake Park Region, to a chain of lakes in the Kandiyohi area. Another venture led him farther north, where he purchased land and attempted to resettle his family in the Sauk River Valley, not far from the site that would one day boast the nation's most famous Main Street.[4]

In each foray, Whitefield coupled a romantic absorption in lake scenery, sometimes depicted with exploring parties camping and cavorting along the shore, to a pragmatic interest in land promotion schemes. As an artist, he pronounced that a country where lakes abounded could not be other than "interesting and agreeable." As a land speculator, he promoted the Sauk River Valley as "The Farmer's Paradise" and Kandiyohi as "The Land of Promise," soon— he thought—destined to be the political center of a new state.

The artist proved the greater prophet than the entrepreneur. Repeated attempts by the

Lake Lillian, Kandiyohi County, *watercolor by Edwin Whitefield, September 1856*

Kandiyohi Townsite Company to win the state capitol failed, and Minnesota's first agricultural boom took off farther south. But the surpassing beauty of Minnesota lakes and streams—and their abundance of fish—would within the next generation lure waves of travelers off of the fashionable river route and through every Minnesota area he painted. None of his land schemes proved to be so well-grounded as his simple declaration that "by the sparkling water of Fairy Lake, on the banks of Minnetonka, or within sight of the spray of St. Anthony's Falls will summer residences be erected."[5]

However prophetic the optimism of Goodhue and Whitefield might prove, Minnesota at midcentury still had a long way to go. Even had the territory not been

Minnehaha Falls and Henry Wadsworth Longfellow in a frequently reproduced engraving of ca. 1875

so distant, placid bodies of water exerted little drawing power for the fashionable tourist. It was the thrill of the sublime, a sense of awe before the mighty spectacle of nature, that put artists on horseback, made adventure a fashion, and enthralled the popular imagination. Mountains met all the requirements of the sublime; so, too, did the vast expanse of the ocean and the torrential leap of cataracts. But the crystalline water and tree-studded shorelines of typical Minnesota lakes, however charming they might be, fell short of the sublime.

Whitefield's modest sketches aside, early depictions of Minnesota generally went along with the prevailing aesthetic by focusing on Minnesota's most dramatic geographical features. After the Civil War, prominent members of the Hudson River school of painting, which was as close to an academy of sublimity as either side of the Atlantic was to produce, journeyed up the Mississippi to paint the mysteriously shaped bluffs below Lake Pepin, the ragged torrent of St. Anthony Falls, and the dramatic river escarpments below Fort Snelling. Even

Whitefield made his woodcut of Minnehaha Falls the centerpiece of his Minnesota Land Agency advertisements, and the popular press followed suit with line-cuts of tourists standing or sitting casually at the base of the mighty torrent.

However graphically they were portrayed, these promises of wild and distant beauty were not enough to lure more than an occasional fashionable tourist north in the 1850s. A second enticement had to be added: a resort equipped with all the civilized pleasures of the city left behind. Like the European spa, the destination of the trip had to abound with good food, first-class service, and abundant opportunities for social life. If it had any hope of competition with its eastern peers, the wilderness resort also had to promise curative baths of mineral salts.

The seasonal community at Saratoga Springs, located a few miles from the Hudson River in upstate New York, had set the tone and scale for eastern watering holes since the 1820s. Its seaside equivalent was the sprawling summer suburb of Newport in Rhode Island.

With the advent of railroads, the principal routes through the Catskill and Adirondack Mountains in New York and the White Mountains in New Hampshire proliferated with upscale resorts cast in much the same mold, each evolving into playgrounds for the wealthy. Widely read guidebooks, such as Bachelder's *Popular Resorts and How to Reach Them*, steered countless pleasure seekers to the mammoth hotels, succession of cookie-cutter villas, and medicinal springs of the mountain summering spots or, if a "cure" from natural ocean salts were desired, to similar amenities on the eastern seaboard.[6]

For many years, every attempt was made to make Minnesota fit the mold of fashion, or at least appear to do so. As early as 1853, with statehood still five years away, Minnesota's premier pamphleteer, John W. Bond, claimed "we have springs equal to any in the world." Like Goodhue, he aimed his pitch at southerners. "Gentlemen residing in New Orleans," Bond continued, "can come here by a quick and delightful conveyance, and bring all that is necessary to make their living comfortable the summer months, and

at a trifling expense. For a small sum of money they can purchase a few acres of land on the river and build summer cottages."[7]

Bond's eye was on the Falls of St. Anthony, which he believed would some day "rank with Saratoga, Newport, and the White Mountains as a place of resort." Seven springs gushed from a nearly perpendicular rock face just below the village that shared the name of the waterfall. All that remained for the resort to take its proper place, according to Bond, was the completion of railway connections to Milwaukee and Chicago.

St. Anthony did not have to wait even that long. A grand hotel, the Winslow House, arose in 1856-57, and immediately proved Bond a prophet by attracting throngs of aristocratic summer tourists from the South. Two freshets of the Chalybeate Springs nearby were said to contain all the properties necessary to restore a torpid liver and a flagging circulatory system. All day long, fashionable southern women promenaded down a path arched with grapevines to partake of a sip of the elixir, a moment's rest on rustic benches, and a panoramic view of river, falls, and

prairie. The men, in the meantime, exercised their fishing rods in the nearby lakes, introducing to Minnesota the split social pattern typical of Adirondack camps and of the state's own summering communities to come.

Extraordinary in scale and cost for so remote a location, the Winslow House sank as rapidly as it rose. At the first mutterings of war between North and South, the lower Mississippi tide receded. The unspoiled

"Summer Life," a popular engraving of summer cottages at Shelter Island Park, Saratoga Springs, ca. 1870

A newspaper advertisement for the Winslow House in 1857

beauty of the site also waned, as erosion and commercial development reduced the falls to a debris-pocked cascade. But the Winslow House paved the way for the grand Minnesota resorts of the late 1870s and early 1880s. More broadly, it initiated widespread interest in Minnesota as a summer destination and spurred additional excursions into the lake region west and north of St. Anthony.[8]

With the sudden demise of the Winslow House, Frontenac, a settlement at the head of Lake Pepin on the Mississippi River, emerged as the next "Newport of the Northwest—the site of the hotels and summer residences of the future." Its claim to such a title revolved around the social instincts and economic ambitions of a single man, Israel Garrard. In the fall of 1854, Garrard left Kentucky for the wilds of Minnesota on a hunting trip and was so impressed with the beauty of Lake Pepin that he took up a tract of land several hundred acres in extent, running for over seven miles along the shore. Three years later he secured purchase of the land as half-breed scrip and immediately set about building a hunting lodge. That galleried mansion, named "St. Hubert's" after the patron saint of hunting, formed the hub of a colony of cottages.[9]

Though railroad publicists and tourism promoters puffed Frontenac as a summer resort well into the twentieth century, it never acquired anything approaching the social glitter, let alone the national repute, of Newport. The residents themselves, led by General Garrard, chose a quieter course when they forced the railroad line connecting Chicago and St. Paul in the 1870s to run west of town. Many who stayed at the lodge or its dependencies were friends or military acquaintances of Garrard, numbering among them such public figures as actor Joseph Jefferson, popular novelist (and general) Charles King, the preacher Henry Ward Beecher, and singer-actress Marie Dressler.[10]

The qualities that set St. Hubert's Lodge apart from fashionable eastern resorts marked the path that Minnesota summer residence development as a whole would take. Cottages springing up around it in the 1860s were at first tied to the social activities, and even the eating schedules, of the main

St. Hubert's Lodge, Israel Garrard's house at Frontenac, in 1972

lodge, but as the complex expanded it slowly evolved into a decentralized community of private summer residences. In the following decades, many of Garrard's visitors made use of their stay by scouting out summer properties at purposely remote distances from St. Hubert's Lodge.

For all of the attempts to force the Minnesota experience into the preconceptions of fashionable travelers, it was the scenic quali-

ties of the lakes that ultimately won them over. As summer cottages began to proliferate along the shores of the larger lakes, their new residents typically maintained a strong connection to the natural surroundings. Like Israel Garrard, many came to the state to find and hold a piece of untrammeled wilderness. They would have relished a comparison between their bucolic life-style and the cynical description of eastern resorts offered by the popular, New York-based *Frank Leslie's Illustrated Newspaper*:

There is no change but a change for the worse in the way many of us spend the Summer. Instead of reading newspapers and backbiting our neighbors and flirting and cackling in the city, we get up and spend a good deal of money in getting away to some uncomfortable place where we follow the same profitable course of life, and profess that we are laying up health and renewing ourselves by contact with Nature. Contact with a fiddlestick! Very few of us care two cents for the open country, or the woods, or the seashore. What we do care for is the genus homo, *like ourselves, with the varnish of city life.*[11]

Minnesota's early lake resorts were not without precedent, however. At midcentury, wandering sportsmen and wilderness enthusiasts regularly spent weeks in the Adirondack wilderness with nothing to fill their hours but hunting, fishing, or just plain sitting. The most famous summer settlement of this sort was the Philosophers Camp, where such luminaries as Ralph Waldo Emerson,

"Summer Life on Lake Chautauqua—Architectural Contrasts," a popular 1879 engraving

James Russell Lowell, and Louis Agassiz communed with nature in the late 1850s, two decades before the mountain routes bristled with pleasure palaces belonging to the likes of J. P. Morgan.[12]

After the Civil War, increasing numbers of remote mountain resorts in New York and New Hampshire offered a quiet wilderness experience akin to the ideals of Goodhue and Whitefield. The first generation of Minnesota

lake cottages in fact clearly echoed already common Adirondack types. One terminological difference stood out, however. Back east, all summer residents were referred to as campers and their shelters as camps, however elaborate the architecture. The wealthy and the fashionable were every bit as keen on maintaining a show of wilderness exposure as they were on dragging their life style with them. In the self-consciously uncultured Northwest, affectations took the opposite turn. Camping was for tenters, while even the crudest of shacks was called a cottage or villa, the two terms being used indiscriminately if not interchangeably.[13]

The tent was the most primitive form of shelter, but life in and around it, even in the rugged Northwest, might be anything but a primitive experience. In Minnesota as in the Adirondacks, colonies of tents often preceded resorts at the larger lakes and held on as a popular option among all classes of people even as more permanent structures became available. Tents could be pitched anywhere permission was granted and rent paid, and rural landowners welcomed the

A tent encampment at Lake Minnetonka, ca. 1890

The "Camport," a portable summer home manufactured by the Open Air Cottage Company, displayed at 162 Virginia Avenue, St. Paul, in 1910

opportunity for extra income. For those planning only a night or two, tents afforded the additional advantage of allowing large parties of friends, church groups, social clubs, or business associates to sleep, eat, and amuse themselves in close proximity to each other yet well apart from other signs of human civilization.

After the turn of the century, in a sort of wilderness echo of the bungalow movement, several tent manufacturers attempted to extend their hold on the upscale market. One St. Paul manufacturer promoted his elaborately engineered patent tent as an "open air cottage." Intended to offer a portable alternative to the picturesque wood cottage,

in practice it compromised one of the key virtues of tent camping by requiring wagon cartage to the site. It was the last gasp of high-fashion lakeside tenting. As small parcels became increasingly available for purchase, camping lost ground to cottaging, and the tent returned to its earliest use among tourists—as a simple, highly mobile

A cottage on Bald Eagle Lake in 1897

Cal's Cabin Camp on Lake Bemidji, ca. 1925

shelter for sportsmen, outdoor enthusiasts, and those for whom high fashion was either unaffordable or undesirable.

The simplest cottage type retained much of the essential form and feel of the natural canvas tent. It was little more than a gabled rectangle sheathed in vertical boards, their seams closed by narrow battens. A window, two at most, adorned the sides, while a flimsy porch grew out from the gable end. In the most primitive examples, the porch literally reproduced the extended entry flap of the tent. Whitewashing the cabin to preserve it brought it even closer in appearance to its forebear. As with the tent, the entry afforded the primary means of ventilation as well as its tenuous tie to whatever social activities lie outside.

Cottages built in this manner continued to spring up at lakeshore sites well into the twentieth century, the only significant changes being additional windows and a substitution of other types of siding. Artistic expression first crept onto the porch, which could boast an ornamented canopy, a formal grid of openings, or millwork elaborated in the current style. Motor lodges of the 1920s and 1930s raised serial editions of the tent-cottage to the status of an icon.

A second summer cottage type sprang from materials available on the site and traded on whatever vernacular was at hand. In the Adirondacks, that meant a log cabin of almost haphazard form, with a canopy or porch built of unmilled tree trunks and sticks. The old vernacular tradition for this kind of construction in the eastern mountains was obviously lacking in a state so new that summer travelers might be the first white men to camp or build on a given lake. Only the birch-bark summer lodges of the Ojibway, many of them still remaining in the heavily forested regions of Minnesota, offered a local prototype with deep traditions. These, however, were far too imbedded in the waning Indian culture. To the white settler, they were simply picturesque relics of an antique and alien culture with little relevance to his summer cottage needs.

Log cabins *were*, of course, built by many of the state's early settlers as their first fixed dwelling. But as a popular option for

An anonymous artist's view of a year-round home in the Adirondacks, 1884

Remains of Ojibway summer lodges near Gull Lake Biological Station in 1893

recreational building, they had to await a period in which log construction had ceased to be a necessity. Only in a few isolated northern outposts did the first generation of residents use unmilled logs for summer cottage construction. The unusual form of some of these seasonal dwellings suggests that they, like the Adirondack log cabin, derived from a vernacular source, quite possibly the summer houses of their builders' northern European country of origin. Finns in particular showed an early and persistent preference for log lakeside retreats, along with a great deal of skill in executing them.

Finnish pioneer Aleck Maki and friends at the Maki cabin on Crooked Lake in Itasca County, ca. 1905

Among the increasing number of wealthy cottagers at the lakes, neither of these first two types of summer dwelling quite passed muster. Tentlike structures and vernacular cabins equally failed to allow for the roomy, well-appointed interiors to which the city-based traveler was accustomed. Worse yet, their lakeside elevations were too short to carry the spacious, open porches and outlook towers known as belvederes seen everywhere on the great summer lodges. Responding to these concerns required a third type of summer cottage, one that adapted the new architectural styles of the suburbs to rustic conditions.

The first summer cottages of this type were generally identified as "Swiss" or "Gothic." They carried a steep, sweeping roof, rustic, Adirondack-style porches, and, if the owner fancied it, an abundance of sticklike decoration. Though the terms were often used interchangeably, the "Swiss" label was more likely to be attached to a cottage if it had overhanging balconies, a roof that swayed outward, or a profusion of pierced wooden ornament. Modern historians use the term Stick Style to cover the suburban equivalent of these picturesque cottages.

Scores of rusticated Stick Style dwellings once adorned several of the larger Minnesota lakes, especially in the vicinity of the Twin Cities. They have not weathered changes in fashion or use very well, in part because so much of their floor plan was taken up by scantily supported porches. But such descriptions, sketches, and fragments—and one intact house—as have come down to us reveal a wonderfully expressive melding of natural settings with urban habits. Exposed framing timbers, applique stick work, and treelike porch braces all harmonized with the woods embracing the cottages, at the same time calling for the use of sophisticated milling machinery. And the broad porches themselves were equally exposed to nature and human concourse. A house that was two-thirds verandas and galleries, surrounded by houses of a similar character, implied a good deal of social interaction, however woodsy its appearance.

Stick Style architecture in its lakeside setting was a bit of a hybrid between its subur-

The "Swiss" Stick Style Charles P. Noyes cottage on White Bear Lake in 1885

ban prototypes—which never really caught on in Minnesota—and the folk construction of upstate New York cabins. The rustic furniture often associated with it was even called "Adirondack," and in the 1870s and 1880s no summer porch in any style was deemed complete without the requisite pseudo-folk assembly of bent and carved branches into chairs and lounges. One local manufacturer, R. L. McKenzie of Excelsior on Lake Minnetonka, boasted a clientele in 1876 that in-

cluded the major hotels of St. Paul and Minneapolis as well as several lakeside resorts.[14]

Closely related to the Stick Style in its dual embrace of urbanity and rusticity was the Shingle Style. The dominant architectural mode of the great mid-1880s Newport Beach resorts, its natural union was with the ground rather than the trees. Not only did it stress long horizontal or diagonal lines, its typical specimens rested on a conspicuous boulder foundation. By 1900 every region of

The Shingle Style Sylvester M. Cary cottage on Manitou Island, White Bear Lake, ca. 1892

the forest. Owners and builders grappled with this limitation by affixing second-story galleries to the lake elevation or overcame it altogether by raising a belvedere high above the roofline. The open corner tower of the Stick or Shingle Style cottage became as visible a mark of the lakeside community as the vast porches fronting its great summer hotels.

Upon the demise of sticks, shingles, and boulders as carriers of artistic meaning for the wealthy, Minnesota cottagers turned to whatever new historically inspired architectural fashion the winds blew in from the East. These were far too diverse to constitute a fourth type. In fact, the high-style cottage was really a retreat from seasonal, environmentally responsive architecture altogether.

With the importation of site-neutral suburban styles came an increased emphasis on lake exposure. The builders of lavish late Queen Anne or colonial revival summer villas invariably cleared the property between the house and the water, with the dual purpose of opening up broad lake prospects and showing off their estate. Only so much of the

C. B. Thurston—C. H. Johnston cottage in Spring Park, Lake Minnetonka, in the 1890s

Minnesota boasted houses built in this fashion, many of the more elaborate examples serving as seasonal lake cottages.

All of these early cottage types responded specifically and even eloquently to their natural surroundings. The summer lake residents of this period—or at least those who settled apart from the great lodges—prized the woods as much as the water. Cottages sat well back from the shoreline, and the intervening trees were allowed to stand; typically, a view from the ground floor balconies gave only glimpses of water through woodland setting survived as could be incorporated into a landscaping scheme that set off the house in much the same manner as the planting scheme of the suburban lot.

The proliferation of this type of suburban housing along the lakes in fact reflected a much more fundamental change than architectural style or even attitude toward nature. It marked the gradual embrace of the larger lake communities by the life of the nearby city and a transition to year-round lakeside residency. Whether the neighboring urban community was as stable as St. Paul and Minneapolis or as subject to seasonal fluctuations as Detroit Lakes and Alexandria was of little consequence. The nineteenth-century lake cottage gave way to year-round use, was engulfed by a larger house, or disappeared altogether.

Alongside this process of absorption or obliteration of first-generation lake cottages occurred a resurgent interest in the very types of summer dwellings that were being swept away. As the Craftsman movement infiltrated into Minnesota, hordes of summer cottage builders at lakes that remained

Design for Charles L. Hoffman's Minnetonka bungalow by Downs and Eads, 1910

beyond the reach of suburbia beat a nostalgic retreat to the simplicity of planks and logs. Many of Minnesota's most distinctive lake cottages date from the climactic years of this period, when the automobile first opened vast areas of the North Woods to extensive migratory settlement. Numerous more recent efforts to give a distinctly modern shape to summering on the lake often owe a conscious debt to these revisitings of the hunting and fishing shack and the primitive log cabin.

MINNETONKA
A LAKE FOR POETS AND PLEASURE SEEKERS

Looking upon the lake from the forest-clad peninsulas and highlands,
its irregular shores and sky-tinted waters present pictures of such beauty as artists
love to paint and poets to dream over. . . . The swinging hammock, the rustic seats,
the screened verandas of the cozy cottage, all speak of comfort, luxury, and rest.

Guide and Directory of Lake Minnetonka, Minnesota, 1884

LAKE MINNETONKA lies at the threshold of Minnesota's vast Lake Park Region. Situated twenty miles due west of St. Anthony Falls, it initiates an unbroken stretch of lakes some hundred miles to the west and twice that far north. Proximity to the Twin Cities was an obvious boon to early cottagers, but the lake displays an abundance of other virtues. Its shorelines dodge and dart into two dozen bays, comprising an east-to-west distance of ten miles and a jagged circumference variously estimated at two to three hundred miles.

R. M. Bennett summer house at Northome, ca. 1895

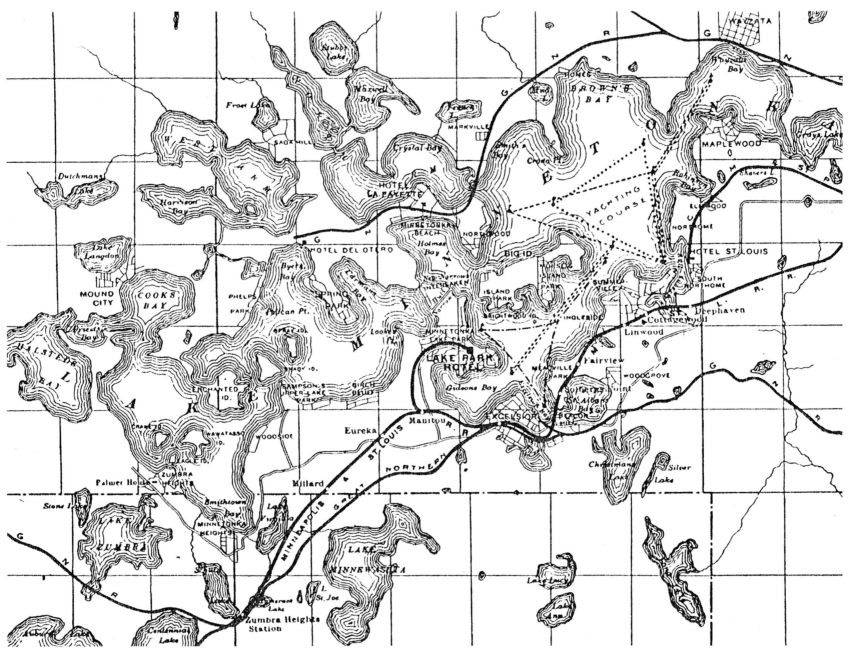

Lake Minnetonka in 1892

Twenty years after the demise of the Winslow House, Lake Minnetonka emerged as the greatest tourist draw in the state, and its day was just beginning. In the late 1880s, at the peak of its summer glory, its shoreline and the embankments above boasted more than five hundred seasonal dwellings and a dozen finely appointed hotels. Minnetonka has also enjoyed a surfeit of recorders and chroniclers since the earliest days of white settlement. More publicly accessible information—both written and pictorial—survives on the history of its summer enclaves and communities than for all of Minnesota's other lakes together. Fortunately, much of that information, particularly what can be painted onto broad historical canvases of seasonal land use and evolving building types, can be applied to the other lakes as well. In its general lines, the story of Lake Minnetonka has been replicated many times over, albeit on a smaller scale, by the unfolding of summering possibilities at lakes throughout Minnesota.

Situated in the heart of the Big Woods, Minnetonka had to be reached at least four times by exploration parties of white settlers before its existence stuck in the popular mind. The first recorded sighting of the lake occurred in 1822, when three young boys from Fort Snelling (including commander Josiah Snelling's son, Joseph, and a drummer boy, Joseph R. Brown) followed the creek up from Minnehaha Falls to its source. But like many of the explorers to follow, they stumbled onto a single bay without realizing that twenty others remained hidden behind it.

Thirty years and several wilderness treks later, the size and unusual scenic values of the lake finally made a public impression. In April 1852, Simon Stevens and Calvin Tuttle set out from the village of St. Anthony for Gray's Bay (where Minnehaha Creek begins), this time walking across the ice through the next bay to the great island in the middle of the main body of water beyond. The *St. Anthony Express* trumpeted their discoveries in a pair of stories published on April 16.[1]

Before the year passed, grand tours of the Upper Mississippi River began to feature the lake on their itinerary. Indian lore added a mythical dimension to its appeal, much of it gravitating around a knob of land jutting into the second (now Wayzata) bay. Long held to be sacred to the Dakotas, its central icon was a magnificently painted boulder. One of the first tourists to arrive on the spot, a physician from St. Louis, promptly pillaged the sacred artifact with the aid of a local farmer. As the brightly painted relic made its way from St. Paul to Pittsburgh to Washington, D. C., an increasing number of curiosity seekers heard of the magnificent lake in the Northwest that had so recently been frequented by Indians.[2]

In August 1852, a month after this invasive piece of propagandizing, New Yorker Elizabeth Fries Ellet arrived, the first Easterner to organize an expedition to the lake for the sake of pleasure alone. Anxious to find the spot where the sacred stone had been located, she and a friend mounted the height of the narrow peninsula, named it Point Wakon (meaning "spiritual place") in deference to its historical significance, and gazed west and south across the main expanse of water. The book that ensued,

Summer Rambles in the West, devoted twenty-two pages to the Minnetonka venture.

A locally organized pleasure party brought John H. Stevens, newspaper editor John P. Owens, and several other St. Anthony village dignitaries to the lake in September, leading to two feature articles in Owens's paper, the *Weekly Minnesotian*. In the following year, Governor Alexander Ramsey himself visited the lake, took a reading of its economic potential, and officially affixed to it one of its Dakota names, "Minnetonka," meaning "big water."[3]

The favorable reports brought back by the Stevens and Ramsey expeditions encouraged a flurry of settlement along the two most accessible shorelines, Wayzata rising on the north and Excelsior on the south. From the outset these were year-round communities, based more on the economic value of the forests and farmland that surrounded Lake Minnetonka than on the recreational potential of the lake itself.

Tourism finally began in earnest when the St. Paul and Pacific Company laid tracks through Wayzata in 1867. Soon after the

THE

CENTRAL RAILROAD OF IOWA

VIA ITS

SOUTHERN RAILW'Y CONNECTIONS

Is the Route to take from all points

East, South and West of St. Louis

To reach the

HEALTHFUL
SUMMER
RESORTS
— OF —
MINNESOTA

Especially the beautiful water-board cities,

ST. PAUL AND MINNEAPOLIS,

and the unequalled

LAKE MINNETONKA

With its three hundred miles of shore, its hundred Fairy Islands, and over one hundred square miles of pure deep water abounding with fish.

Railroad advertisement published in 1877

railway came lake steamers, allowing visitors to travel readily across the water from town to town and bay to bay. Yet the distances were still too great and the lake transportation too erratic to permit the establishment of summer residences. Prior to 1875, only Moses Guild and the Gale brothers, Samuel and Harlow, built cottages exclusively for summer use, and for many years the latter used their lake homes for so little of the season that they functioned primarily as rental lodges.

Samuel and Susan Gale's summer occupancy of Lake Minnetonka land dates to the mid-1860s, when they preempted a bulging stretch of shoreline a short walk south of Point Wakon, or Spirit Knob as the lake residents called it. Gale originally visited the area in 1864 after stopping over in Wayzata to deliver a pro-Lincoln speech during the president's campaign for reelection. In 1869 he and Susan erected their first cottage and dubbed it Rustic Lodge.

The Gale cottage was a simple gabled and whitewashed board-and-batten structure not far removed from a tent in form or sophistication. Intended from the first as a place to entertain parties of friends, Rustic Lodge soon had wings of similar structure and began to function as a boardinghouse. In 1876 it was fitted up as a summer resort and renamed the Maplewood Inn, with the Gale family taking rooms until selling the enterprise and building a new cottage in 1880.[4]

Samuel Gale's prominence as a Minneapolis real estate agent, financier, and civic leader and his wife's popularity in social circles brought many visitors to Rustic Lodge. Within a few years, a half-mile-long colony of summer cottages and clubhouses began to stretch from Spirit Knob, by then familiarly known as Breezy Point, to the Moses and Sara Guild place, with the Gale cottage at the center. This was the first nucleus of private summer residency on a Minnesota lake.

A long and often-iterated tradition notwithstanding, the Gale cottage was actually not the first summer structure to be built on Minnetonka. The Guilds had preceded the Gales by two years, purchasing a large parcel of land from Susan Gale in 1867 (when the Gales were still summering in tents) and building immediately. Sara Guild was a schoolmate of Susan's in Pittsfield, Massachusetts, and, according to one account, had induced her husband to move into a wilderness area to combat his drinking problem.

Samuel and Sarah Gale cottage after its expansion and conversion to a hotel in 1876

They immediately put up a cabin of squared oak logs, attaching roof and flooring without the use of nails.[5]

Unlike their neighbors of the 1870s, the Guilds regarded the log cabin as their primary residence, though they wintered in Minneapolis. They were the first of many to operate what amounted to a small, subsistence farm above the lakeshore during all but a few months of the year. The fact that they were not vacationing may account for the tendency of Minnetonka journalists and historians to overlook their cabin's claim to priority. Moses and Sara Guild were also outsiders who never established a place in Minneapolis business or social circles. Finally, they built a type of dwelling that failed to pass muster as a lake cottage in Minnesota of the 1870s and 1880s. For the hordes of wealthy Minneapolis and St. Louis travelers who would swarm to the lake in its years of glory, a log cabin was a throwback to pioneer days and not a proper summer cottage at all.[6]

Though the upper echelons of society never embraced its owners, the Guild property became a favorite strolling and picnicking spot for lake travelers. Seats and swings were scattered through the woods and on lake overlooks near their cabin, and a croquet court enhanced the front lawn. Moses and Sara served up a profusion of berries from their own gardens, along with fried fish, chowder, and ice cream. Their simple estate, called Wildwood, gave a more intimate view of lake life than Maplewood just north of it and played its own part in addicting future cottagers to the charms of the lake.[7]

Before any of the Gales' or Guilds' visitors set up their own lake dwellings, Samuel's

Samuel C. Gale in 1891

brother, Harlow, established a unique summering spot on a bit of land poking out of the water just below the largest island in the lake. He first visited the tiny island, scarcely more than an acre in extent, in 1863, so he preceded Samuel as a Minnetonka tourist; but various legal conditions surrounding the

preemption of the land on the island kept him from surveying and purchasing it until 1872. In the year following his purchase he put up an octagonal summer house said to be modeled after the home of writer J. G. Holland on the Connecticut River.

Holland's plan must have been liberally interpreted, for the cottage had only three rooms, two on the first floor and one above (later divided into two), with no provision for cooking. A porch wrapped the ground floor, and a picturesque exterior winding stairway led to the second. Painted red, the cottage was called Brightwood. A bathhouse and an icehouse fronted the beach below it. Gale paid $2.85 for the land and by 1876 was renting the island out for twenty-five dollars a week when his family was not there, receiving a handsome profit on his investment while he continued to use it at his pleasure.[8]

If roughing it was part of that pleasure, the Harlow Gale family must have been happy indeed. All slept on straw ticks, women on the second floor and men on the first. Periodically the ticks were taken ashore for fresh stuffing, then rowed back

Harlow Gale family and friends at Brightwood, ca. 1885

summer went by without occupancy of the island by several hundred renters and other visitors. Successive additions to the main structure jutted out from the sides and rear, but the faceted lake view remained intact until Brightwood was demolished after three generations of use.[9]

Hardly had the Gale brothers settled into their wilderness retreats when the northward migration of Southerners, put on hold during the Civil War, began again. Foremost of the new summer residents was Charles Gibson, a St. Louis attorney and statesman of national stature; best known among his many honors was a commendation from the King of Prussia, leading to various attempts by his friends to attach a "Sir" or "Von" to his name. Gibson was no stranger to the lake. During his frequent stays at the Winslow House in the 1850s, he had taken a horse and buggy to Excelsior and explored many miles of the Minnetonka shoreline.

No year-round citizen of the state was more impassioned about the healthfulness of its climate or the beauty of its lakes than Gibson, and none invested so deeply in the

on a dead calm day, precariously balanced astride two row boats. A cow was kept on the island, and getting it to swim out every spring was one of the highlights of the summer for the children. Though she swam well, the cow hated all the prodding and would occasionally flop over on her side and float, snorting and rolling her eyes as if she were dying.

In the 1880s a three-story boathouse, complete with workshop, additional bedrooms, and a belvedere, joined Gale's other beachfront structures. By that time Brightwood regularly entertained large parties, and not a future of Minnetonka. During one of his visits, he purchased a quarter section of land on a broad, elevated peninsula a mile south of Breezy Point. After he, his wife, and their six children spent several summers camping on the shore in the early 1870s, he built a landing, cleared the brush at the highest point of the property, and hired Minneapolis architects Long and Haglin to design the "neat and comfortable" Gothic cottage he would call Northome.[10]

Begun in September 1876, Northome's startup cost of three thousand dollars was modest for a man of Gibson's wealth and standing. He was quite clear about wanting to "enjoy the delights of the lake without being compelled to submit to the requirements of fashionable foibles." But in its final form, spread out over a forty-by-seventy-foot plan, Northome dwarfed all other summer houses on the lake for many years to come. Its two-level veranda, extensive plumbing system, and multiple stone fireplaces set the standard for the lake's better class of summer houses until the neoclassical manor houses of the early 1890s.[11]

Like many of the first-generation cottagers, Gibson located his summer home well up from the shore, in the midst of the dense woodlands that filled his property. But as the primary force behind the establishment of Forest Park in St. Louis, he was well aware of how the landscape could be shaped to serve both naturalistic and human ends. While planning for the cottage was still underway, he called in a Boston firm, commonly believed to be Olmsted and Company, to lay out his tract. Three broad avenues were cut through the forest, two of them exposing the cottage to lake vistas and the third opening a prospect to the rising summer sun.[12]

For Gibson as well as the state's official promoters, Minnetonka was the gateway to Minnesota's natural splendors. Around it lay ten thousand more lakes whose exploration had just begun—more than two lakes apiece for each of Minnetonka's annual tourists, as Gibson observed in 1878. The occasion of Gibson's remark was the granting of a charter to the Minneapolis and St. Louis Railroad for a line connecting the two cities. William

Charles Gibson in 1876

D. Washburn, the president of the line, had pushed the authorizing bill through the Minnesota legislature, then organized a lavish reception for the combined elite of St. Louis and Minneapolis at Northome. In the lead after-dinner speech, Colonel Swayback spoke for the St. Louis contingent in declaring that "the Minneapolis and St. Louis Railroad only hastens the period when from the maple crowned cliffs which are all about us, dwellings furnished with all modern conveniences and comforts, pleasanter places than the castles upon the Rhine or Danube built in [other] centuries by a feudal ancestry for their emperors, will stud the border of the wonderful lake like gems upon the diadems of nature."[13]

In the wake of Gibson and the Gale brothers came fifteen years of intensive cottage-building activity, sponsored as much by tourists from Missouri, Iowa, Chicago, and even New York City as it was by the affluent citizenry of Minneapolis and St. Paul. But the Maplewood area remained in the hands of local men. In 1876, Wayzata area farmer George Woolsey erected the lake's second octagon house, a peculiar-looking affair that was subsequently remodeled, moved, and remodeled again. An avid gardener and fruit grower, Woolsey was said to have the best strawberries in Minnesota. Cozy Nook, Minneapolis homeopath P. L. Hatch's cottage, went up the following year, and it was cloned by flour miller George Washington Crocker's Glenwood in 1879.

The Hatch and Crocker cottages were among the first Stick Style structures on Lake Minnetonka. Like the dozens of others

Gibson's belvedere, ca. 1900, the only fragment of his summer estate to survive into the twentieth century

Breezy Point Lodge, ca. 1885

erected between 1879 and 1883, they were devoid of ornament except for the porches themselves and the treelike brackets that supported a variety of roofs. Breezy Point Lodge, a clubhouse built at the base of the historic promontory in 1879, was the most prominent cottage of that character. Established by six Minneapolis businessmen, the Breezy Point Club met an early demise because of its rule that any of the group who married would forfeit his membership.[14]

The sudden influx of Easterners and Southerners in the late 1870s restarted old comparisons between Minnesota resorts and posh Eastern establishments. A reporter from Fergus Falls was so impressed with the handsome new cottages and finely outfitted pleasure steamers that he believed that Minnetonka was "fast becoming acknowledged as the Saratoga of the West." A more local writer warned hotel keepers that visitors who had a short time ago sought out the simple comforts of a rural retreat were coming to expect "the magnificence and luxuries of a watering place." Along with the self-congratulation came a certain amount of

droll humor, more often than not directed at out-of-state visitors. Mrs. E. R. Eldrige of Decatur, Illinois, met with such luck at fishing and dining that "her live weight is fourteen pounds more than it was two weeks ago." A pair of New York ladies staying in Wayzata were said to be "very fat and very knowing"; they had, after all, "spent summers and summers at Saratoga and Long Beach, and they had been abroad."[15]

Two of Gibson's Northome visitors, George Jackson of St. Louis and T. A. Harrow of Louisville, pooled their resources to build the first grand resort hotel on the lake in 1879. Located in the midst of 215 acres of forestland that Gibson had added to his original holding, it was first known as the Harrow House. But the Kentuckian wanted more than this stake in a St. Louis enterprise and left to establish his own hostelry on a remote Upper Lake island. In 1880 Gibson himself took over the hotel and promptly renamed it the St. Louis.

For the first time, there was a facility on the lake capable of entertaining large numbers of guests in grand style, and wealthy

Southerners flocked to it. Some cities, like Memphis, sent a virtual colony north to spend the summer. The hotel could accommodate four hundred guests, no rooms were smaller than twelve-by-eighteen feet, and each suite had gas, water, and its own entrance to the verandas.

And what verandas they were. The hotel extended 215 feet across a wide cutting in the forest that was open to the bay, its wings carried back another 127 feet on each side, and the porches adorned three stories of each façade. Setting the pace for all future hotels and villas, these vast open-air galleries were the site of daily lake gazings, nightly balls, and pacings to and fro all hours of night and day while wives waited for their husbands' return from fishing, sailing, and partying. Aside from the sweep of the porches, the hotel's exterior was plain almost in the extreme, a long gray rectangle with sparse green trim. But boxlike simplicity was the standard for summer hotel architecture of the 1870s, even in the most fashionable of the Adirondack or White Mountain communities.

St. Louis Hotel, ca. 1885

Rather than competing with private cottage owners and developers, the St. Louis Hotel added to their number. Numerous visitors ultimately sought summer accommodations of their own on the lake. Gibson also sold off much of the property belonging to the hotel for cottage lots in the late 1880s. So many Minneapolitans summered on former St. Louis Hotel land that it came to be known as the West End, fancifully connecting it to the city ten miles distant.[16]

On the north-facing slope of Carson's Bay, well below the Gale and Gibson properties, another development sponsored by Samuel Gale lay waiting for an opportune moment. Gale platted Cottagewood in 1876, the same year that he turned his summer house into a commercial enterprise. But it was destined for quite a different clientele from Maplewood or the St. Louis. The land was densely wooded, but the lots were small and without remarkable features. What the lots along the shore *did* have was a sloping grade perfectly suited to boating.

In the late 1870s, the interior lots began to fill. As early as 1879, several dozen summer cottages were up and in use. Three years later, wealthy cottagers began to buy up the choicest lots along the water. This time the pace was set by two men from Kansas City, L. T. and L. R. Moore, who hired Minneapolis architect Carl F. Struck to design a cottage and several outbuildings for them to share. Initially the boathouse cost nearly as much as the dwelling, but then a succession of remodelings set in. Superb millwork, fine interiors, and full gas and plumbing made Cresthaven "one of the most complete villas" on the lake. Minneapolis merchandiser William Donaldson purchased the Moore villa in 1892 at the unheard of price of forty thousand dollars. That sale was the largest residential real estate transaction at the lake in the nineteenth century.[17]

Cresthaven gazebo in 1990

Carl F. Struck in 1891

Struck quickly became the dominant architect of Cottagewood and its neighbor to the southwest, Summerville. In 1885 he designed a second cottage for a Kansas Citian, Judge T. A. Gill. The *Northwestern Tourist* declared "there is not its like for beauty of architecture on the lake," though it had the small scale of the typical Cottagewood house. Four cottages for Minneapolis families followed in quick succession, Struck's own among them. Each was gaily decorated with patterned shingles and fret-sawn ornament.[18]

With the outstanding exception of Cresthaven, Cottagewood houses tended to show substantially more exterior elegance than interior finish. Rufus Jefferson, grandson and namesake of one of the original cottagers, remembered many of the most impressive exteriors to be little more than fronts for walls of bare studs. Interior decorating consisted of pinning pictures onto the back side of the sheathing. It must have been a matter of priorities rather than economy, for the lakeside cottagers included numerous men of wealth from Minneapolis and St. Paul, all of them avid yachtsmen. Hardware

Thomas B. Janney cottage and boathouse, ca. 1902

in the mid-1870s was its freedom from the noise and bustle of railroad travel. Excelsior also had the distinction of being a dry town, removing another source of disruption to the quietude of summer evenings and weekends. Visitors were assured of not being kept too far "out of the world" by the availability of a morning newspaper, either the local *Lake Minnetonka Tourist* or one of the Minneapolis papers, a few hours after it was printed.[20]

Minneapolitans E. A. Harmon and Mrs. C. S. Clark were the first to build summer homes in Excelsior. Their cottages of 1875 served quite different purposes. Mrs. Clark's Topside soon evolved into an enclave of small rental cottages (twenty by twenty-four feet was standard), while E. A. Harmon used his as a post for scenic tours. He kept a horse and wagon ready, leading the local newspaper to report (perhaps facetiously) that he regularly "runs up between weeks to breathe the inspiring atmosphere of our lakes and the sweet odor of flowers on the hillside."[21]

Other early summer cottagers were wholesale druggist George R. Lyman and

wholesaler Thomas B. Janney and lumber dealer Rufus Jefferson were among the most prominent. The latter built a two-story boathouse as well as a playhouse for his daughter, Dora, that attracted considerable attention.[19]

With the growing popularity of camps and cottages along the eastern bays of the lake, the town of Excelsior at the extreme southern end began to attract attention as a vacation community. Its particular charm flour and lumber miller William D. Hale. Lyman was the first president of the Minneapolis YMCA and an advocate of the simple life, at least in short doses; his descendants would bequeath the second Lyman summer estate, a log lodge east of Excelsior, to the organization he founded. To their ranks were added many other Minneapolitans engaged in the flour milling business, among them Frederick C. Pillsbury, A. H. Bovey, and Llewellyn Christian, who rented or bought cheap cottages at Excelsior while casting about for sites on the lake that held a longer term promise of seclusion from urban life.[22]

Soon out-of-state entrepreneurs began infiltrating the booming cottage market in Excelsior. Joseph and Carl Pockett of Winchester, Indiana, put up their Little Brown Cottage in 1878. It quickly mushroomed in size and capacity. Tourists from Iowa flocked to the community, and an enterprising Iowa City businessman obliged them with Iowa City Park, a cluster of summer houses that grew from a crude cabin to more than twenty "permanent" (that is, enduring more than a few years) residences in 1881.[23]

Iowan contributions to summering on Lake Minnetonka reached a peak in 1879 with the construction of the Lake Park Hotel on a broad peninsula above Excelsior. Its governing body, the Minnetonka Park Association, consisted of three Minneapolitans and two Iowans. Its staff also included two musical directors from Iowa. The association set out to establish a resort very much like that of Chautauqua, a famed Adirondack summer community that began with a program of Bible study and campfire singing and grew to include assemblies on a wide variety of religious, literary, and scientific subjects. Like the Chautauquans, the association was an outspoken opponent of the unrestrained social life that infected most of the better resorts of the day:

The design of the Minnetonka Park Association is to furnish those who have no taste for dissipating pleasures a place for summer rest where, besides the allurements of a beautiful lake and the most charming natural surroundings, there should be added such moral, spiritual, intellectual, aesthetic and social attractions as would draw together people of literary, scientific or religious tastes, for the mutual benefits and delightful recreations afforded.[24]

Minnetonka visitors apparently had little stomach for so stringent a fare. After an inaugural season of Sunday school assemblies, temperance meetings, and a musical convention, the association sold out to a group intent on seeing the Lake Park Hotel become a pleasure resort vying with the St. Louis across the lake. Lake Park continued to host such events as spiritualist camp meetings and Christian Endeavor Society assemblies, but it could no longer claim a consistent purpose separating it from the increasingly worldly social life of the lake as a whole.

The hotel's design, created by Minneapolis architect LeRoy S. Buffington, was remarkable only for its statistical accomplishments. Running 420 feet along its main axis, the building sported seven belvederes and multiple tiers of verandas that completely encircled the structure. Its rotunda could accommodate an assembly of three thousand people, and its dining hall had a capacity of five hundred.[25]

The Lake Park Hotel contributed to Minnetonka cottage development in quite a different way from its east-side competitor. Instead of hosting a well-to-do clientele that would eventually seek out land on their own, the association directly offered lots for sale or rent on its extensive holdings on the peninsula. Initially the entire plat of Lake Park was divided into double lots, with a stockholder owning one-half of each lot. The purpose of this arrangement was to prevent the emergence of land-hogging summer estates or, even worse, the accumulation of large parcels of land by a single owner for speculative purposes.

Failure of the outlying lots to sell under these stringent conditions probably helped speed the collapse of the association. But the unusual platting of the park close in to the hotel led to a loose community of summer residences unlike anything else at the lake before or since. Laid out in the fashion of an English garden by Minneapolis civil engineer

Frank H. Nutter, it encouraged both lakeside and forest development. Three distinct arrangements emerged: one circling the shore around the boot of the peninsula, another hidden within the forest, and a third lining a strip of lakeshore above the hotel, confusingly known as West Point. Most of the cottages were small and unpretentious. The single outstanding exception was General T. L. Rosser's villa on the north shore of the peninsula, designed by Minneapolis architects Kees and Fisk and said to be the largest cottage on the lake after Gibson's.[26]

The hotel itself struggled almost from the beginning. Cheap construction and an awkward design may have mattered little to the members of the association, but those coming for pleasure alone expected at least the affectation of culture. The hotel's one sustained claim to fame was its kitchen and dining hall, which served private cottagers and boaters as well as hotel guests. It boasted a French cook and a service staff of college students. The latter innovation was advertised as "the very best of white help," a non-too subtle dig at the St. Louis habit of

Lake Park Hotel, from a sketch by one of Buffington's draftsmen

bringing black waiters and kitchen crew north for the summer.[27]

While cottage building was booming on the eastern and southern bays of Lake Minnetonka, the north end was barely getting started. The St. Paul and Pacific connection to Wayzata was early and effective as a means of bringing tourists out to the lake, but the town itself suffered from the arrangement. The rails ran the length of its main street, marring its prospects as a resort community (among other things) and provoking a long and bitter battle with James J. Hill, the majority stockholder in the railroad.

A stretch of the lakeshore west of Wayzata held the most promise. Steeply embanked along its length and terminating in a narrow, rocky point, it answered the needs of those who were looking to establish a quasi-wilderness summer fiefdom. First to plant his family on the bank was Julius H. Clarke, Minneapolis agent of the American Express Company. Every evening Clarke would join his family at their Marian Cottage, then return to work by the morning train. Like the Gale place across the lake, Marian Cottage

drew large numbers of friends and business associates, but Clarke was not well enough placed in Minneapolis society for his summer residency to inspire ripples of development around it.[28]

Far more important in establishing the rising social character of the west side of Wayzata Bay was the invasion of Lookout Point by four prominent Minneapolis families linked by blood as well as business. In 1877 the three Christian brothers of Minneapolis milling fame joined with C. M. Hardenburgh, the founder of the Minnesota Iron Works and related by marriage to the brothers, to purchase the land at the terminus of the west shore. They cast lots for location of their respective summer houses but agreed to hold the very tip of the point in common.

Hardenburgh was the first to build, naming his cottage Blithewood. The best the *Tourist and Sportsman* could say of it was that it was superior to a tent. George H. and Llewellyn Christian followed suit, moving into Heart's-Ease and Sunnyside, respectively, in 1878, with J. A. Christian's Woodbine

Frederick C. Pillsbury summer house, ca. 1890

Cot a year or two behind. Like the Hardenburgh cottage, all were of board-and-batten construction.[29]

The George Christian house soon came to be known locally as The Ramble because of its haphazard expansion through a lateral wing. First came a dining room projection, then a kitchen and storeroom with guest quarters above, and finally, a laundry. A few yards off shore from The Ramble lay a wanigan, a kind of flat-bottomed boat devised for summer quarters by French fur trappers and still being used by loggers. In its Minnetonka setting, the wanigan served as a pirate ship for the children. By all accounts, the men and young folks enormously enjoyed their rustic summers, while the women struggled with long hours alone and the domestic staffs were so overworked that many quit before the season was out.[30]

Not until 1886 did Wayzata Bay gain a cottage that displayed the social standing of the Minneapolis families that were gravitating to the west shore. Frederick C. Pillsbury, another milling giant, hired Minneapolis architect George M. Goodwin to design as full-blown a Queen Anne mansion, at least in outward appearance, as anything in the city. Called simply Lake Home, it cost six thousand dollars, was painted dark green, and exuded gloom to the children that played along the shore. Perhaps profiting from a more distant lake view, a newsman cited it as "the best and prettiest cottage on the lake" when it burned to the ground in 1897.[31]

Goodwin designed a simpler and more companionable Queen Anne cottage for grain merchant Albert C. Loring just to the northeast of the Pillsbury property in 1887. By this time the entire stretch of shore from the highlands southwest of Wayzata to the point was known as Ferndale, a once facetious title for land that boasted neither ferns nor valley. All of the land had been bought

Interior of the Albert C. Loring cottage, from an 1887 sketch by the architect

George A. Brackett and his summer house on Orono Point, ca. 1910

up by wealthy Minneapolitans. It was only a matter of time before mighty colonnaded neoclassical villas in "the Minneapolis" style would gaze solemnly across the bay at the still-rural village and the humbler cottages of an earlier generation.

Beyond Lookout Point, the next projection into the lake bore the mysterious label of Starvation Point on account of a trapper said to have met his end there. Prominent Minneapolitan George A. Brackett purchased the entire peninsula in 1880, built his summer house at the point, subdivided the remainder into large lots, and cast about for a suitable new name for the peninsula. Known for many years as Orono Point after its owner's place of birth in Maine, among local residents it also took on the name of Brackett himself.[32]

A long career in public service had endeared Brackett to the people of Minneapolis. Founder of the fire department, former mayor, and sometime head of United Charities, he had hosts of friends and a summer house large enough to accommodate many of them at one time. On the lake, he was probably best remembered for his bean-hole beans. Two huge iron pots, each sufficient for feeding one hundred people, had followed Brackett from the Civil War and the Dakota War to his tranquil summer retreat. When the Minnetonka Yacht Club was formed in 1889, his land instantly became the home base of the sportsmen and their families during the regattas. At the end of the day, Brackett offered a hayrack ride followed by a bean feed out of his pots, which had been buried in coals for much of the day.[33]

Among the first to buy into Brackett's newly platted property was William H. Dunwoody, a business associate of the Christian brothers on the next peninsula. Around 1890 Dunwoody followed Brackett's lead by erecting a house designed by Minneapolis architect William Channing Whitney. Its interior walls were beautifully sheathed in deeply stained pine boards, creating a mix of elegance and rusticity anticipating the varnished knotty-pine interiors still half a century away.

West of Brackett's Point were two bays separated by a wide peninsula first known

Dining room of William Dunwoody summer house, ca. 1908

as Island City. It was destined to hold a place at the center of Minnetonka's summer life in the halcyon 1880s. The first tract to be developed was Northwood, a triangle of land at the southern tip of its eastern end. Platted by a pair of staunch Baptist churchmen from Minneapolis, W. W. Huntington and A. R. Potter, the land was settled rapidly. Huntington and Potter built a "Swiss" cottage named Buena Vista in 1879, and eight other cottagers followed on their heels.[34]

Northwood was a meager enterprise, however, compared to the grand development scheme that engulfed the remainder of the peninsula. In 1880 James J. Hill saw an opportunity to trade on the success of the two new hotels on the lake and establish a beachhead for his railroad empire at the same time. In short order he extended a Wayzata spur of the newly reorganized St. Paul, Minneapolis, and Manitoba Railway through Island City and began plans for a hotel whose size and opulence would beggar the competition.

The Lafayette Hotel, reputed to be the largest and grandest in the Northwest,

opened to great fanfare in 1882. Running 745 feet from end to end and costing $400,000, its reputation for grandiosity was well warranted, though Easterners might have sniffed at its boasts of elegance. Local newspapers and tourist rags immediately credited the building of the hotel with an "inauguration of a reign of fashion and high life at the lake," and they were not far from the truth. All three of the major hotels on the lake began to hold twice-weekly balls, the Lake Park Hotel boasted concerts by nationally renowned performers, and two more yacht clubs sprang into existence.[35]

Though the hotel drew the nation's attention, the Manitoba Road's platting of the lots around it into Minnetonka Beach ultimately had a far more lasting impact on the development of the lake. With the building of the Lafayette Hotel, all the excesses of the Queen Anne style arrived with fanfare and a flourish, while Minnetonka Beach assured that they would find ample ground to multiply. An enclave of stylish summer mansions arose on the south shore, many of them surviving to the present day.

The most expensive lots in the new development were located just west of the hotel drive. Lumberman George Camp was the first to build on them. In 1884 the *Northwestern Tourist* praised his villa for corresponding well in style to the hotel, while "more taste in colors of paints [were] used in adorning it." Three years later Minneapolis grocer Anthony Kelly put up a tempest of Shingle Style gables and catslides house that made Camp's house appear to be the model of restraint. About the same time, Minneapolis miller F. R. Petit built Alle Riva, a cottage with the steep roofs of the "Swiss" or "Gothic" style of the 1870s but encrusted from head to foot with fretsawn ornament leaping from Gothic to Chinese. Petit had just joined the Christian brothers' firm, and the lake gave him as good a place as any to display his good fortune.[36]

Successive builders on the south shore of Minnetonka Beach called in the best Minneapolis architects, and most of them responded in an adventurous spirit. In 1890 W. C. Whitney, usually the most circumspect of designers, created a 150-foot run of continuously

Alle Riva, the F. R. Petit summer house, in 1983

Horace Henry summer house, ca. 1890

balustrated porches for railroad contractor Alonzo H. Linton's Wyoming Lodge. About the same time, William H. Dennis, the first Minnesotan to profit from a French architectural education, gave another railroad contractor, Horace Henry, a bombast of neoclassical forms and devices, all perilously hung on a Queen Anne plan.[37]

On the north side of Minnetonka Beach, facing into Crystal Bay, the houses kept to more modest proportions. The best of them were imaginative renditions of the Shingle Style, quirky in detail but utterly at home on the site. St. Paul architect Allen H. Stem, a man of extraordinary artistic as well as architectural gifts, created a gloriously romantic cottage in this vein for his family. The Henry Doerr cottage, designed by

Minneapolis architect William A. Hunt, sported a twin-peaked dormer and a broadly curved belvedere. Unfortunately few of these Crystal Bay cottages survived the transition to year-round life on the lake. Many of them, including Stem's, burned within a decade of their construction.

From the arrival of the Gale brothers to the beginnings of an elite lake society at Minnetonka Beach, most of Minnetonka's growth as an extended summer community occurred on the eastern half of the lake, generally referred to as the Lower Lake. The Upper Lake to the west remained relatively unsettled, in spite of a widening of the channel to admit large steamers in 1873. For twenty years thereafter, the Upper Lake continued to draw heavy tourist traffic on account of the unspoiled wildness of its scenery and its numerous picturesque islands. Lakeshore development occurred in isolated patches, and some areas, such as the North Arm and East Arm, failed to establish summer colonies at all until well into the 1880s.[38]

One of the first white settlements on the Upper Lake contributed to its aura of wilderness isolation. In 1855 Frank Halstead, who had come from New Jersey by way of the California Gold Rush, took up a lonely claim on the south shore. After service in the Civil War, he returned to build a one-room, board-and-batten cabin, loaded it with books, and quickly became as much of a tourist curiosity as the wild islands his cabin faced. His obvious learning, air of refinement, skill in building (ships as well as cabins), and death by suicide in 1876 turned his property—duly named the Hermitage—into an obligatory

Allen H. Stem summer house, from an 1889 sketch by the architect

51

George Halstead at the Hermitage, ca. 1900

stop on the grand tour of the lake. Halstead's brother, George, took over the cottage, using the same dishes, furniture, and unusually fine library, but retreated to Excelsior in the winter. By exacting a toll and occasional food from picnickers and curiosity seekers he was able to subsist until fire consumed both him and his cabin in 1901.[39]

Following the Halsteads' lead, the earliest summer cottages on the western bays sought out the most remote locations. Frederick A. Jennings of the U.S. Treasury Department bought a large parcel of farmland on the westernmost extreme of the West Arm sometime before 1874. He put up a cottage in 1876, after which he and his family regularly retreated to the farm in the summer. No record survives of the Jennings cottage apart from an 1876 newspaper report of a "neat, two story building, much better than the average of homes about the lake." According to that same report, his wife and daughter managed the farm, while his son established his own rural retreat a short distance away. Frederick, Sr., apparently gave himself to hosting friends and catching fish.[40]

The West Arm's ambience as picturesque farmland continued to be its principal summer draw well into the twentieth century. Two lakeshore settlements arose in the late 1880s—Saga Hill and Fagerness. Each was operated and peopled largely by Scandinavian-Americans. Saga Hill's settlers were a mix of professionals, ministers, bankers, and professors, most of them affiliated with the Norwegian Lutheran church, particularly the Trinity congregation in Minneapolis. Both West Arm settlements consisted of simple cottages and cabins with a pointedly rural flavor, and this character remained constant so long as the summer communities survived.[41]

In 1875 the largest of the Upper Lake's many uninhabited islands also half-yielded a bit of its wildness to summer settlement. St. Paul businessman and avid outdoorsman Carrington Phelps bought the entire four hundred-acre island and proposed making it into a park with no subdivisions. His intention was to lease spots for tents or knock-down cottages, while maintaining his own summer home on the southern tip. He succeeded in managing the eastern bank of the island in this fashion until the mid-1890s, when Phelps Island Park began to be parceled off for cottages.[42]

From the beginning, Phelps's villa also functioned as a lodge, repeating the pattern of Samuel Gale's summer house at the other end of the lake. In 1887, shortly after the family had moved in, a visitor from the press found them taking tea and eating ice cream out in the grove. He "could not help but think that some of our city friends would be surprised to see how pleasant and happy it was to rough it in the bush, especially where they could have a cow to furnish milk, and a never-failing supply of fresh fish to draw upon, and a store within twenty minutes row."[43]

In the middle of the Upper Lake and almost connected to Phelps Island lay Enchanted Island, believed by many to contain the most beautiful property on Minnetonka. Charles A. Zimmerman, secretary of the Minnesota Sportsman's Association and one of the state's leading professional photographers, purchased the western third of it in 1879. He immediately built a "handsome villa in the middle of a fine grove" and set about landscaping the grounds. In the following year he added a studio, where he intended to put the finishing touches on watercolor studies of the lake.[44]

Zimmerman had hardly completed construction of his island retreat when his only daughter died, driving him and his wife from the island with the resolution never to return. But a second tragedy rekindled his love for the very personal sanctuary his piece of island had become. A devastating fire in 1888 leveled the wooden cottage, and Zimmerman immediately set to work planning an even more ambitious summer villa.

Designed by A. H. Stem, the architect of Zimmerman's St. Paul house, Bowlder Lodge quickly became one of the most celebrated sights of the lake. Its walls were constructed entirely of lake boulders drawn up from the shore by a tram specially built for the purpose. All sizes and tints of boulders were fitted together, and a walkway of the same material linked the cottage to a towered boathouse on the shore. Zimmerman also designed and built a lift bridge connecting his property with Phelps Island.

"Commodore" Zimmerman and Bowlder Lodge, ca. 1901

Hailed as both odd and cozy, Bowlder Lodge and its companion structures effectively expressed many of the facets of Zimmerman's own personality and accomplishments. He was both a man of refined culture and a rugged outdoorsman. To his acclaimed artistic and photographic work he added the vocation of steamboat owner and captain. He and his fleet of lake steamers were so popular a site on the lake that he was known everywhere as the Commodore.[45]

The smaller Upper Lake islands were evenly split between commercial and private use. Dunlop Island and Shady Island went to hotels, while single cottages arose on Spray Island and the diminutive Wild Goose Island. William H. Grimshaw, a minor Minneapolis architect, designed a simple cottage on Spray Island in 1880, intending it to serve for both his family and that of his father, Robert E. Grimshaw. Each man had lost a wife, and their second wives were almost the same age, creating an unusual bond of friendship between generations. Wild Goose Island was a much lonelier place, barely supporting the cottage and

Robert Grimshaw and his daughters, Blanche and Maude, at their cottage on Spray Island, ca. 1900

boathouse erected in the early 1880s by Edward V. Reel of Hawk Farm, Missouri.[46]

As the islands began to be populated, numerous settlements started up on the north and south banks of the Upper Lake. First came Howard's Point, a south-shore peninsula located halfway between the Narrows and the Hermitage. Its first summer occupants were Minneapolis merchant families, who built Oakhurst (1877), Idylwild (1879), and Pleasant View (1882). Immediately below Howard's Point, the colony of

Woodside began with Florida college professor J. H. Pomeroy's villa, and just west of it, resort owner C. W. Sampson subdivided his lakeshore property into Sampson's Upper Lake Park. Through the 1880s, successive colonies formed in ripples away from Howard's Point.

Few if any of the cottages in these small enclaves rose above the level of "cozy and comfortable" ascribed to P. B. Christian's Oakhurst. What distinguished them from Lower Lake settlements was the

Edward V. Reel cottage and boathouse on Wild Goose Island in the 1880s

extraordinary social and geographical diversity of their owners. They were all there because of the lake itself, not because of the social opportunities it offered.

The north shore of the Upper Lake gave rise to a community of quite a different character. In 1881 a group of St. Paul and Minneapolis business and professional associates—many of whom were linked by personal ties—began to buy up property on a 150-acre peninsula known as Casco Point. Led by close friends (and soon to be partners) Chauncey W. Griggs and Addison G. Foster of St. Paul, the group pulled in investors from New York, and these were soon joined by St. Louis natives who had discovered the point while summering at other Minnetonka resorts. By the time the cottagers formally organized as the Spring Park Association late in 1882, at least nine had already built summer residences there.[47]

Among the first were Griggs and Foster, who chose to live together in a vast barnlike structure, its lake exposure wrapped with a two-story veranda. Built in 1880 at a cost of three thousand dollars, its roof called for

Griggs and Foster cottage, ca. 1885

thirty-six thousand shingles. Early predictions that the villa would "have room enough for several people in it" proved to be an understatement. During the summer of 1882 the entire Griggs and Foster families and their inlaws, seventeen people in all, vacationed together at the cottage.[48]

For the first few years, visitors to Spring Park—including New Yorkers whose summer houses were under construction—stayed at the cottages of their St. Paul friends. But the spot became so popular, and its residents had so many friends, that the association had to put up a dormitory to house the overflow. Maids, coachmen, boatmen, riding and carriage horses, and a French chef came north with the St. Louis cottagers. Spring Park became an intensely social colony, all the families eating together in a plainly built but well-appointed central clubhouse. In later years, the son of Spring Park's caretaker gave a farm lad's view of the summer settlement:

The people had a very gay time. They built great big summer houses and boat houses, three storied, some of them were, and for ninety days they stayed. It was never more or less. Sometimes they'd fish early in the morning. And they'd ride through the woods and they'd sail. Sometimes they roped us children fast to the boats and we'd sail in a race with them. And they'd visit and laugh and fall in love—and nothing bothered them.[49]

Charles Johnston cottage, Spring Park, designed by J. Walter Stevens, ca. 1890

Spring Park was unique among Minnetonka settlements in forming a fashionable, closely knit summer colony independent of a major resort hotel. Some of St. Paul's finest architects exercised their skills on the point, among them D. W. Millard, J. Walter Stevens, and Clarence H. Johnston. All had prior connections with the St. Paul cottagers. But as a unified social entity, the colony barely made it into the new century. Many of the St. Louis and New York cottages were bought up by Minneapolitans with no prior association with the original settlers, the clubhouse lapsed into disuse, and conversion to a year-round suburb was inevitable.

In the 1890s, prevailing architectural currents moved in a neoclassical direction far removed from the prevailing rusticity of even the toniest lakeside developments. The turned baluster, giant portico, and pedimented gable became the rule of the day, and architecture at the lake adhered as closely to the new order as the most exclusive sections of Minneapolis.

A stately, suburban form of neoclassicism made its first Minnetonka appearance in the most unexpected of places: the north shore of Morse's Island. Though far and away the largest island in the Lower Lake—its name was gradually changing to Big Island—it remained largely unsettled through the 1880s. Long-time landowner W. B. Morse maintained a campground on the east end; only the western shore had been platted to cottage lots.

At the heart of the island was the finest stand of virgin forest remaining in central Minnesota. It was this property, a parcel of 125 acres, that Olaf O. Searle purchased in 1891 and immediately converted into an estate of fantasy proportions. A three-story colonial revival house arose on the north end of his tract. It boasted steam heat and gas lights, over twenty rooms, and marble-trimmed baths. Searle also installed such amenities as a several-thousand-book library

Olaf O. Searle house on Big Island, ca. 1902

and a mural of a Valkyrie spanning from floor to ceiling.

Like the others who chose neoclassical monuments for their lake homes, Searle regarded nature as something to be improved upon. Vast lawns of mown grass hosted ornamental plantings and opened the way to a Japanese garden. Searle also cut a channel through the island on a north-south line. At its upper end, the channel swelled into a lagoon with an island, which Searle connected to the mainland by a footbridge. To this watery ensemble were added a gazebo, a towered boathouse, and a dock large enough to hold an orchestra for summer evening concerts.[50]

The property and its improvements cost Searle a quarter of a million dollars, but that scarcely made a dent in his business profits from 1891. Ten years earlier, he had arrived in Minneapolis as a penniless Norwegian, but a stint with the St. Paul, Minneapolis, and Manitoba Railway and eight years managing an emigration agency had opened the way to a vast fortune. In the banner year, when he began to spin out his fantasy on Morse's Island, he sold a million dollars worth of passage tickets to America and five million dollars worth of acreage, while maintaining partial ownership of several banks along with substantial investments in North Dakota bonanza wheat farms.[51]

In the late 1890s *Minneapolis Journal* editor Lucian Swift erected a mansion of equal pretension on the west point of Cottagewood. With the Moore-Donaldson estate on Grandview Point to the east, the humble row of Cottagewood cabins and boathouses was now framed by two commanding monuments. The new country seat "rejoiced in the poetical Indian name of Katahdin," but Swift's architect looked to Greece and Rome through Jeffersonian spectacles. At the heart of Katahdin's plan was a circular living hall

Katahdin, the Lucian Swift summer house, in 1898

thirty feet in diameter, and at the center of that space stood that quintessential symbol of the man of leisure, a billiard table. When the hall was used for mixed company, a polished cover allowed the table to double for food service and knick-knack display.

Like the Searle house, Katahdin had a furnace, allowing it to be opened for special occasions in the winter. In a feature article on the Swift estate, the *Home-Builder* magazine opined "there is no place which so lends itself to Christmas festivities [as a country house]; whether nestled between Berkshire hills, or framed in as fair a setting on Minnetonka's wooded shores." As formal parties were one of its intended uses, Katahdin naturally had to be decorated in the latest fashion—the walls and ceiling painted in shades of green with rose decoration, and the false beams accented with gold. According to the *Home-Builder*, "Elegant country houses of this class are now being built every year at Minnetonka."[52]

The most scholarly pillared mansions on the lake went up in the Minneapolis grain merchants' enclave at Ferndale. Numbering

six in all, each was designed by W. C. Whitney, and all were essays in some monumentalist genre of neoclassicism. Whitney's masterpiece was Highcroft, a gambrel-roofed brick mansion in the late Georgian style that commanded two bays from its lofty site. Owned by grain dealer Frank H. Peavey, Highcroft received its name from Minneapolis's pioneer interior decorator, John S. Bradstreet.

Like the year-round properties north and west of it, Highcroft was a working farm. The summer house arose in the midst of open land that continued to be maintained as hay meadows. But the grounds immediately around the house were landscaped to plans developed, at least at the first stages, by F. L. and J. C. Olmsted. The work of Olmsted and Son (as they were more frequently known) was utterly unlike the earlier plan ascribed to Olmsted at Northome. The landscaping of Northome had been based on the carving of prospects through the forest; Highcroft had no forests, and rather than attempting

Highcroft, the Frank H. Peavey summer house, in 1902

to develop one, the landscapers stuck to meandering low plantings, scattered trees, and formal gardens. Nothing was permitted to bar the mansion's sweeping views in all directions.[53]

In a supreme stroke of irony, the three most pretentious Minnetonka summer monuments of the 1890s, each designed to be habitable for winter occasions, shared the same fate as the crude seasonal dwellings of the prior decades. Searle's lonely venture on Big Island ended with the premature death of his wife, the loss of his fortune, and a consuming fire. Katahdin also fell to fire early in the century, and Highcroft was bulldozed in 1953 to make way for a subdivision.

Even without fire or changing land use, the neoclassical giants were doomed from the beginning. It took a ton of coal to get the Katahdin heating system working, and Highcroft required eleven carloads just to make it through the fall season. The ambitious landscaping schemes of all three demanded an owner unusually devoted to horticulture, and none had children of like enthusiasm. Similar problems overcame

Cedarhurst, R. M. Bennett's replacement (to Whitney's plans) of Charles Gibson's estate at Northome. Half-solving the heating requirements of a monstrous house and surrounding it with acres of meticulously man-

aged land was as much of a death warrant as constructing a humble cottage on a tiny lot in one of the outmoded rustic styles.[54]

While a gargantuan neoclassicism had many of the lake's most prominent sites in

Squirrel's Nest, the Frank B. Long cottage, ca. 1892

its grasp, lesser locations closed out the century with a great variety of new looks. Far and away the most original achievement occurred on the Wayzata shore, where Minneapolis architect F. B. Long put up his summer house. Inspired by bits and pieces of houseboats and steamboats more than by anything in traditional summer house construction—let alone architectural style—the cottage had a remarkable formal affinity with the "Houses of Tomorrow" that were still forty years away. The crowning feature of Squirrel's Nest, as Long called it, was a corner staircase to the roof supported by iron rods and enclosed in what appears from early photographs to be wicker.

At the turn of the century, many of the lake's new summer residents opted for a variant of colonial revival that was tainted with the spatial and material effects of the earth-and-lake-bound earlier styles. The colonnaded porch of W. J. Keith's design for John Birkholz at Minnetonka Beach is a particularly clear example. Proper spacing between the columns and a proper skirt around the base are ignored in favor of wide,

John Birkholz summer house in 1904

airy openings and a traditional boulder foundation. Birkholtz also indulged in a Japanese garden, a common feature of turn-of-the-century Minnetonka cottages.

Minneapolis architect George Bertrand was as informed a scholar of the historic styles as anyone in the city, but he also proved adept at compromising for the sake of opening up the house to the summer. Old Orchard on Brown's Bay, built for sash-and-door manufacturer John F. Wilcox, inserted a properly three-part Palladian opening into the forward gable, but made it into a doorway through which the family could pass from their bedroom hallway

to a balcony overlooking formal gardens and the lake.

With the explosion of summer housing styles and types at the turn of the century, Lake Minnetonka settlements—Ferndale excepted—began to lose their individuality. Even so homogeneous a community as Cottagewood, sandwiched between the two pretentious estates on the points, lost its unities of scale and orientation as replacement housing introduced building types that had nothing to do with lake-gazing or boating. The design signatures of specific architects and builders rather than the general character of a settlement became the determiners of

Old Orchard, the John F. Wilcox summer estate, in 1905

Harry Wild Jones in 1891

whatever visual cohesiveness remained. This pattern was hardly unique to Minnetonka; it is the universal experience of one-dimensional communities taking on a more multi-faceted life.

One area of the lake resisted loss of its historic wooded lakeshore identity more than any other. The stretch of land between Northome on the north and the bottom of Carson's Bay on the south, all currently identified as Deephaven, continued to be a magnet for summer architecture that had the feel of indigenous character well past World

War I. The leading architect of the area was Harry Wild Jones of Minneapolis, and it was his distinctive sheathing of sophisticated modern plans with rugged natural materials that set the tone for Deephaven.

Jones's first clients on the lake were prominent members of the Minnetonka Yacht Club, and their clubhouse of 1890 was among his finest achievements. Five of the yacht club members also called on him to design private cottages, though only two actually executed them according to his plans. Even the humblest of Jones's designs was endowed with gracious interior spaces quite unlike any the lake had seen. The William T. Rolph cottage, for example, exposed its sticklike framing members in the old Adirondack fashion, but the house within radiated from a two-story octagonal hall.[55]

A much larger house built for Sarah Passmore incorporated the foundation of a boulder-faced cottage of the 1880s, but also drew occupants into the house through a nearly round entry hall. Jones also designed a number of secondary structures, such as a monumental entry arch for the George Gil-

lette summer estate. Most made conspicuous use of lake boulders or dark-stained shingles.

Even W. C. Whitney, ordinarily the most style-conscious of architects, contributed to the environment-bound character that the east shore began to acquire in the last decade of the century. In 1892, across Carson's Bay from Cottagewood, he designed a boulder-and-shingle cottage for Minneapolis clothier and avid yachtsman Hazen J. Burton. Called Chimo, the house was the first year-round

George Gillette entering his summer estate, ca. 1915

Glooskap in 1891

Drawing room, Walden II, ca. 1912

architect Howard van Doren Shaw to design a house for him. The Georgian manor had become pedestrian on the lake; what Douglas wanted and got was an eighteenth-century Franco-Italian palace surrounded by formal gardens.

In a fashion typical of nineteenth-century industrial magnates, Douglas named it Walden II, after Henry David Thoreau's crude pond-side retreat that had come to symbolize the simplicity of a life without money or possessions. This latter-day Walden had brocaded walls, Gobelin tapestries, a ceiling copied from an Italian palazzo, and a morning room decorated in French period style.[56]

After Douglas went down with the *Titanic*, his wife Mahala carried forth at Walden for another thirty-three years. The preeminent party maven of Minnesota, her guests included Presidents Harding and Coolidge, Marshall Foch, and Gertrude Stein. "Life is glorious and beautiful and fun," she wrote, "and I intend to get and give my share." A diminutive woman, she hired Harry Jones to design a teahouse for her,

lake residence for a Minneapolis commuter. Behind the main house, Whitney also created two cottages for the Burtons' summer guests, the most fanciful of them named Glooskap after an Indian spirit.

Two pre-World War I designs by Chicago architects, both built on land first developed by Charles Gibson, crystallized the differences in taste and sensibility the wealthy brought to the lake after the turn of the century. In 1906 Cedar Rapids, Iowa, resident and Quaker Oats heir Walter Douglas purchased the remaining St. Louis Hotel property, tore down the long-vacant relic, and commissioned Chicago society

Walden II, the Walter and Mahala Douglas summer house, ca. 1912

Francis B. Little summer house, ca. 1920

and he responded with one whose doors and windows were scaled to two-thirds their normal size. Even Jones's contribution to the estate mirrored the self-contained aesthetic of the Douglases. The house and its grounds were art objects that created their own environment; where they were built was of little matter.[57]

While the Douglases were conferring with van Doren Shaw, Peoria lawyer Francis Little sought out Frank Lloyd Wright to design a summer house for him in a corner of Northome, less than a mile from Walden II. Wright openly detested his fellow Chicagoan's work, and a more different approach to the Minnetonka setting could not be imagined. Offered the chance to mount a house on an uneven hilltop,

Wright split the crest further and nestled his design over and within the fold. Two hundred fifty feet long and glazed with three hundred leaded windows, the Little house made an artistic statement as strong as Walden II's without lording over its woodland environment. In fact, Wright tried to work the natural setting into an ornamental program by inserting triangles of bright green glass to suggest aspen leaves into the great banks of windows, but Little held him to a purely geometrical scheme.[58]

However current public sympathies may seem to have vindicated Wright's organic view of the relationship of house to grounds, the history of the Douglas and Little estates plainly did not. Walden II still stands proudly on its bluff, while the Little house fell to the wreckers in 1972, the victim—among other things—of the monstrous costs of heating it when a succeeding owner chose to winter there. Another splendid Prairie School design, Purcell and Elmslie's Edward Decker house overlooking the east shore of Wayzata Bay, succumbed to the same fate and for much the same reason.

Living room, Edward Decker summer house, ca. 1912

Year-round houses on the lake continue to exploit the historical revival styles and site-sensitive options with equal fervor. When left to their own devices, builders tend to design in a current suburban style, oscillating between colonial revival and something akin to French Renaissance, with the site having nothing to say about the matter. Architects, on the other hand, have made it a showplace of modernist versions of life in nature, from woodsy post-Wrightian retreats to vast walls of glass.

WHITE BEAR
A PEARL SET IN EMERALD

*There are a dozen minor summer resorts around about
St. Paul and Minneapolis, but White Bear Lake is the resort.*

MARK TWAIN, *Life on the Mississippi*

*White Bear has pavilions, club houses and pleasure boats galore. But it has never
become noisy and Coney-Islandised. It remains today a place for rest and pleasure rather
than rioting and boisterous sports. It is fashionable without being fashion-ridden;
popular and populous without being crowded.*

Northwest Magazine, July 1885

EIGHT MILES NORTH of St. Paul lies a lake as different from Lake Minnetonka as
St. Paul is from Minneapolis. Lake Minnetonka is all bays and promontories and islands;
White Bear Lake is a broad sheet of water broken only by a single isle and two lone
peninsulas. It presents a unitary picture of quiet beauty, accessible at once and from all
sides, rather than a series of ever-changing vistas that invite exploration and discovery.

The road to the depot in Dellwood, with the A. M. P. Cowley cottage in the background, ca. 1890   71

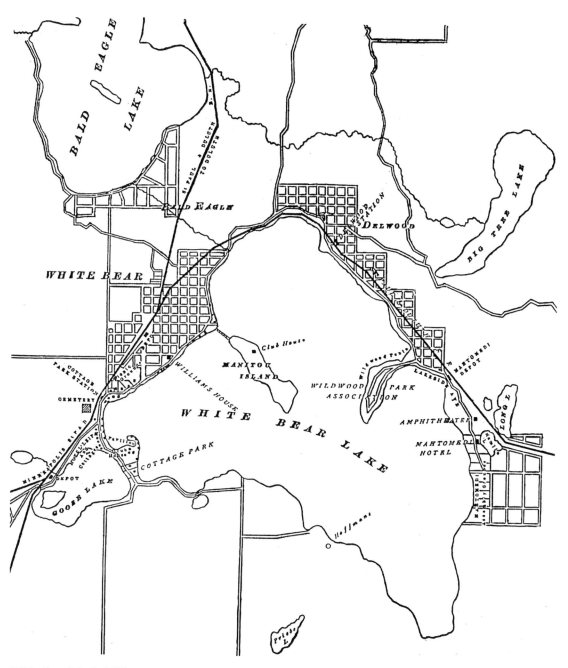

White Bear Lake in 1883

The openness of the lake perfectly mirrors its historic ease of access to people of all social classes—again in stark contrast to the lake west of Minneapolis.

White Bear rarely inspired the sort of side trips that took easterners to Minnetonka on their grand tour of the Upper Mississippi. Perhaps its dearth of narrow waterways or sudden, spectacular vistas deprived tourists of the sense of mystery and awe they expected of wilderness experiences. The lake also lacked Minnetonka's connection to the Mississippi River and the lore of Minnehaha Falls. Whatever the reason, White Bear first came to public attention through purely local efforts and without a hook to the national touring constituency.

In the early days of the territory, the lake's most vocal champion was James Goodhue, editor of Minnesota's baptismal newspaper, the *Minnesota Pioneer*, and tireless promoter of all that the near and distant environs of the city had to offer. Goodhue first set his florid pen to depictions of the White Bear area in the summer of 1850. His initial focus was on the farmland about it and its great advantages to easterners and British immigrants. A year later, on July 22, 1851, Goodhue reported on what may have been the first purely recreational outing on the lake by white settlers. "A picnic party of 14 or 15 ladies and gentlemen went out last week to White Bear Lake, ten miles north, and spent a day very delightfully at fishing and hunting." This event took place a year before Elizabeth Ellet's bold excursion to Minnetonka and more than ten years before mixed outings would begin to occur there.

Finally, in 1852, Goodhue toured by horseback to view the glories of the lake for himself—and find an occasion to vent his well-exercised passion for superlatives. From the vantage point of the Barnum homestead on the west shore, he extolled the charms of the body of water before him, "extending for miles, surrounded with gently swelling hills, covered with trees, and the whole shore lined with pebbles [of] all colors, including some very beautiful carnelians. In the midst of the lake, like a vast flowerpot, is an island so crowded with rock maples trees, that you can scarcely see to read by daylight. . . . The surrounding lake is fairly rippling with millions of finny inhabitants."[1]

What made both the picnic of 1851 and Goodhue's jaunt of 1852 possible was a road cut through to the lake from St. Paul. The venturesome could now rent horses and carriages from a St. Paul stable and travel the ten miles in two hours. A resort business soon followed. Goodhue's host, Villeroy Barnum, enlarged his cabin to welcome paying guests in 1853. Four years later, an elegant Greek Revival structure complementing Barnum's crude hostelry arose. The Murray House catered to those seeking undiluted indolence, while under a new owner, Barnum's hotel reoutfitted as a sportsman's resort. By the time the Civil War broke out, White Bear Lake had become a popular spot for holidays and weekends, even siphoning off some of the eastern and southern traffic that flowed to the Winslow House for the curative airs and cool waters of a northern climate.[2]

At the close of the Civil War, about the time that the St. Paul and Pacific Company tracks pushed through Wayzata, the St. Paul and Duluth Railroad built a line that would serve as the major conduit between White Bear Lake and St. Paul for the remainder of the century. The tracks skirted the western shore, and a spur to Stillwater continued the circuit along the northern side. In 1879 a branch of the Minneapolis and St. Louis Railroad connected the White Bear depot to Minneapolis as well. Lakeshore entrepreneurs vigorously responded to the new opportunity. The old Barnum Hotel was upgraded again, this time as the Leip House, the Murray Hotel became the Williams House, the South Shore hotel sprang up just below the Leip House, and the building of the depot spawned the White Bear Hotel, a picnic pavilion, and a restaurant for travelers.

Three of the hotels added cottages in the 1870s. Initially built as a cheap way of handling overflow, the detached units became a popular first choice among an increasing number of wealthy tourists. A boom in private cottages ensued, leading to the creation of a succession of communities along the upper two-thirds of the lake. By 1882 a continuous road connected all of the summer enclaves, from Cottage Park and the village of White Bear on the west side, then around the north and east shores of the lake to Dellwood, Wildwood, and Mahtomedi. The dense growth of timber between road and water was systematically thinned, opening the cottages to the sun and a glimmer of the lake.[3]

From the outset, west-side White Bear cottagers enjoyed a distinct advantage over their Minnetonkan peers. The journey to Minnetonka in the 1870s was long and arduous, even with one leg of the trip provided by the train to Wayzata. Except for residents of Wayzata itself, cottaging at the lake was impossible for any who had to work in the cities. It was either a total vacation for all or a summer stay for the mother and children while the father lived in the city and came out on weekends. White Bear, by contrast, offered a rail connection twenty minutes from downtown St. Paul and a few minutes walk from the west shore of the lake. As a writer for the *Northwest Magazine* observed, "A man who lives upon St. Anthony's Hill in St. Paul, or any of the outlying residence sec-

tions of Minneapolis, in the winter, finds the summer trips from the lake to his office no longer than he has been accustomed to all the year round from his home in the city."[4]

In spite of its practical advantages for the St. Paul resident, White Bear was still not quite positioned to compete with Minnetonka. Through most of the 1870s, tent camping "with all the accessories of rowing, sailing, fishing, hunting and out-door life generally" set the tone for lakeside life. The town in 1876 still had only two hundred permanent residents, and the hotels had little to offer but a room and meals. Settling in for the summer, with a full family in tow, was a lonely affair, particularly in contrast to the scale and variety of social life available to the patrons of Excelsior and Wayzata hotels.[5]

Because of its proximity to the depot and the two oldest hotels, the west shore was the first to develop a cottage community. As early as 1876, at least four privately owned cottages crowded a small stretch of Lake Street below the hotel grounds. Belonging to the St. Paul families of Dr. J. H. Stewart, H. P. Hall, E. B. Gibbs, and Walter Mann, what

they looked like has been lost to public record. One thing we do know is that they and many like them had neither stove nor fireplace. Residents took their meals at the Williams House. At least one west-shore cottager, Major Pratt of St. Louis, also used the Leip House to extend his vacation. When his summer house became too cool for comfort, he took up quarters at the hotel, stubbornly remaining at the lake until it froze over.[6]

In the late 1870s St. Paul's elite finally began to gravitate to the west shore of White Bear Lake. Leading the way was a group of closely linked families that had been fixtures at Minnetonka hotels. As they began to purchase contiguous lake property at White Bear, microcosms of St. Paul society sprang up independent of the resorts. George R. Finch, vice-president of Auerbach, Finch, Culbertson and Company was the first to tear himself away from Minnetonka. In the fall of 1877, he purchased a White Bear lot near the Williams House and began to build a cottage, moving in with his family the following summer. In mid-1879 the cashier of Finch's company, H. A. Boardman, built a "neat cottage to cost about $2,000" nearby, and they were soon joined by new neighbors—but old friends of Boardman's—the Charles P. Noyes family.

Next in line came cottages for William R. Merriam and Walter Mann (possibly a replacement of his earlier cottage), the chief officers of the Merchants National Bank, in 1880. Merriam was a long-time summer vacationer at the lake. As early as 1860 he had joined with White Bear residents and tourists—including Pittsburgher and future cottager T. C. Fulton—to organize a Union Sunday School. Finishing off the north end of the cottage row in 1879 was a "snug little structure" built for St. Paul Harvester Works president Charles Corning and his family.[7]

The Merriam cottage had the most stylistically advanced design of the growing west-shore enclave. Planned by St. Paul architect LeRoy S. Buffington, it was the first example of the Queen Anne style at either lake. But in expense and popular acclaim, Buffington's effort was easily outstripped by a design from an unknown hand, the "handsome and unique Swiss cottage" of C. P. Noyes. Six

Charles P. Noyes cottage in 1997

years after it was built, when Noyes and his brother Daniel (whose family shared it with Charles's family) had moved on to larger quarters in a more secluded setting, White Bear publicists continued to single the cottage out for special praise. Said a writer for the *Northwest Magazine*, the cottage "is very tastefully built on a site which breeds envy and hatred and all uncharitableness in the mortal who sees it. There are many tantalizing residences upon the lake, but few if any are so tempting as this one of Judge Young's [the second owner]."[8]

By 1881 the string of cottages on either side of the Williams House had become a landmark of the community. A local writer described them as "a large number of elegant villas, owned by wealthy businessmen of St. Paul, who send their families here to reside in the summer and join them each evening after the close of business." A biographer of C. P. Noyes attributed his ability to work steadily through the summer months to this daily respite from the heat of the city. But the Noyeses and their neighbors did not remain long on the west shore. As quieter

and more exclusive areas of the lake were platted, St. Paul's elite relocated, and their original cottages fell prey to redevelopment. The "Red Chalet" of the Noyes family is the lone survivor of the first great burst of summer house building at White Bear Lake. But the town could have done worse, for the Noyes cottage is also the most elegant standing specimen of the Stick Style in the state.[9]

Proximity to the railroad depot, which had served the west shore so well in the 1870s, became a liability to those who came to the lake for solitude in the 1880s. According to the *American Travelers Journal* in 1881, the white tents of campers were so crowded together that "the shores during the heated term present much the appearance of a mighty army." In the same year, Newson claimed that White Bear had reduced camping to a science, several of its encampments having achieved the size of villages and the individual tents "being as comfortably and even luxuriously furnished as their bedrooms and living rooms at home."[10]

As if these tent cities were not enough, the hotels along the lake built bandstands,

dance arenas without walls, and saloons, each introducing its own distinctive crowds and noises to the western shore. The Leip House, by then usually known as the Hotel Leip, could accommodate hundreds of dancers and nearly one thousand diners spread between rooms at the inn and canopied outside pavilions. The social shortcomings of White Bear Lake had been remedied with a vengeance.

Late in 1881, the chartering of the Cottage Park Improvement Association and the Manitou Island Land and Improvement Company signaled the birth of White Bear Lake communities that were carefully designed to assure privacy and a modicum of tranquility. Cottage Park occupied a sixty-acre peninsula on the south side of the lake just around a bend from the populous west shore. In the spring of 1882, the land was "subjected to such changes in surface aspect as will make it conform to the ornate ideas of a landscape maestro," the conductor of the moment being A. D. Hinsdale, a St. Paul architect not otherwise known for his landscape planning schemes.

Family and friends at the Frederick Willius cottage, ca. 1885

After toying with the city's best-known architect, E. P. Bassford, the association retained D. W. Millard, a recent but well-credentialed arrival from Chicago, to design the central building. Millard followed the program of the exclusive, male-dominated community clubhouses on Lake Minnetonka, placing reception and dining rooms at ground level and billiard and gaming rooms above, confining women and children to the lower floor. Kitchen and sleeping quarters for the service staff occupied a separate building.[11]

Members of the Cottage Park Association were expected to build "no abodes but those of wealth and refinement." They responded by hiring St. Paul's leading architects. The first builders, St. Paul grocer P. H. Kelly and banker Frederick Willius, called on Bassford, who gave them cottages in a sprawling version of the Stick Style shorn of any Swiss artifice. They were closely followed by E. N. Saunders, who hired George Wirth to design a cottage "in the approved lakeside style"—whatever that might mean—on a prominent site at the western end of the development. If Wirth's Summit Avenue designs of the same period are any indication, the Saunders cottage was probably as densely detailed as any in the new development for some time to come.[12]

The fifth architect to be commissioned at Cottage Park was a brash, artistically obsessed twenty-five-year-old of scant reputation. Early in 1884 St. Paul railway solicitor Reuben B. Galusha hired Cass Gilbert to design a cottage for his family, and the young architect served him well. The spreading gable, long second-story window ribbon, and finely crafted porch addressed the street with dignity, while open galleries to the rear and an abundance of exposed rafter timbers melded the cottage into its natural site. Cottage Park would never acquire a more stirring design; indeed it had little opportunity to do so, as the finest lots were restricted to a half-mile bulge of east-facing shoreline that was largely taken up by 1886.[13]

Manitou Island underwent rapid development within the same time frame as Cottage Park. It first came to state attention in 1851, when a logging survey led to the extraction of its heavy timber by Stillwater lumberman Jonathan McKusick. But by the 1870s, it was once more a flourishing and idyllic woodland spot, host to myriad picnickers and parties of campers. Tales of the island's sacred import to both the Dakota and Ojibway—who fought many times over occupation of the lake—led to its early name among white settlers, Spirit Island. Its developers romanticized the name further by reverting to the Dakota equivalent, "Manitou."[14]

Late in the summer of 1881 Stillwater lumberman D. M. Sabin and thirteen prominent

Reuben B. Galusha cottage in 1997, its colors altered to historic hues

St. Paul businessmen led by William R. Merriam banded together to purchase the fifty acres of land on the island. Sabin's stake in the development was probably purely financial—a grant of rights to all timber cut in the process of laying out the roads and building the cottages. The St. Paulites, on the other hand, plainly intended to spend their summers there, as each built a cottage within the next several years.

Once the purchase was made, the new owners of the land incorporated as the Manitou Island Land and Improvement Company. The capital stock of one hundred thousand dollars was divided into two thousand shares with a par value of fifty dollars. On the board of directors were seven well-placed St. Paul men: William B. Dean, Charles Noyes, R. M. Newport, and W. R. Merriam—all of whom had built cottages on the west shore—and three newcomers to the lake, C. H. Bigelow, E. F. Drake, and F. B. Clarke.

To plat the island, lay out roads, and provide for landscaping that would shape and supplement its already lush growth, the association hired the Midwest's preeminent landscape gardener, Horace S. Cleveland. The plan that ensued created a road of three sequentially linked loops, the first loop to contain the clubhouse and the last to encircle a lagoon that would be used as a shared marina. While the roads were being laid out, the finishing touches were applied to the "ornamental" bridge that would unite the island to the mainland.[15]

With the completion of the bridge and roads in 1882, several Manitou Islanders set about building their cottages. Like the Cottage Parkers, they hired the best talent in St. Paul. Among the first buildings to be completed was a clubhouse planned by J. Walter Stevens. It had a billiard room, bowling alley, dressing rooms, and full-length verandas along with the sitting room-dining hall that was its chief reason for being. A large kitchen anchored one end of the building, the intent of the association being to provide meals to all of the islanders.[16]

In the spring of 1883, three cottages in a row were begun on lots at the front of the clubhouse circle. All designed by Clarence H. Johnston, an architect still in his early twenties, they reflected the latest eastern trends in woodland resort building. James A. Wheelock, editor of the *St. Paul and Minneapolis Pioneer Press*, got a properly upright Queen Anne, its lake exposures deeply carved with long verandas and loggias on the first and second floors. For business partners and friends S. M. Cary and Paul H. Gotzian, Johnston produced imaginative variants of the Shingle Style, in which prospects from the house appear to determine the plan of both the lake and road elevations. Upon its completion, the Gotzian house was justly praised as one of the finest cottages in the Northwest.[17]

Four other cottages begun in 1883 or 1884 established the reign of the Shingle Style on the island. Charles Noyes built his second cottage at White Bear in the squarish, hip-roofed form of a recreational pavilion, while S. J. R. McMillan and former Minnetonka habitué E. F. Drake opted for picturesque composites of irregular masses with multifaceted or semicircular porches. As Clarence Johnston received three unknown White Bear Lake commissions beyond those already

Paul H. Gotzian cottage, ca. 1892

cited, these may have been them. Close on the heels of Johnston's commissions, and almost certainly finished before any of them, was H. S. Treherne's smaller but equally artistic design for Judge E. C. Palmer, notable for its magnificent arcaded veranda.[18]

The efforts of early Manitou Islanders to settle into their new retreats were constantly thwarted by prolonged construction schedules. With the single exception of the Palmer cottage, whose two-thousand-dollar price tag was less than half the norm for the island, these first houses took two and even three summers to finish. Many of the families camped out while their cottages were being built, first in tents, then in partly completed areas of the house. The Cary family, for example, was reported to have moved into their cottage in July 1883, though it was not finished for another two years.[19]

By 1886 Manitou Island was well on its way to becoming the most exclusive summer enclave in the state. Eleven cottages were already up, and the south end and most of the northeast bank still remained virtually undeveloped. The owners' association had spent thirty-five thousand dol-lars on the landscaping, roads, bridge, and clubhouse, and individual cottage owners had collectively more than matched that amount. On Lake Minnetonka, only nine summer houses built before 1886 had cost as much as four thousand dollars, while the eleven on Manitou *averaged* five thousand dollars apiece.[20]

The first generation of Manitou Island residents lacked the strong business and social interrelationships that so often characterized lake colonies of the period. Indeed, the island was for many a refuge from the social burdens of city life. Even the shared eating arrangement proved to be so unpop-ular with island residents that the catering service was discontinued after two years. The architects of the first cottages had pre-pared for this exigency by providing kit-chens in their plans—a rare feature of sum-mer houses elsewhere on the lake.

Treherne's design for Judge Palmer fol-lowed a common summerhouse expedient by exiling the kitchen to its own building with staff or guest quarters overhead. But most if not all of the cottages planned by Johnston placed the kitchen in the basement of the cottage itself, with food delivered via dumb waiters. The reasoning behind this novel arrangement was unimpeachable. Social mores dictated that the kitchen of any dwelling, whether urban or rural, be located away from the street side, lest it fill the halls and parlors with unwanted odors. But on the Manitou location, placing the kitchen to the rear would block or shorten a full view of the island setting. Putting the kitchen in the basement was the only solution short of building a separate structure.[21]

Just as Clarence Johnston was the domi-nant Manitou Island architect of the 1880s, the 1890s belonged to Cass Gilbert. In his hands, the association's already distin-guished legacy of Shingle Style architecture was assured of a lofty continuation. Most of his clients were on the upper half of the northeast coast. The first, Walter S. Morton, built a cottage joining an enormous gambrel-roofed mass with boulder piers and walls. It became a part of island lore when the second owners, the William F. Peet family, erected a brass pole to the boys' rooms on the third floor. When the boys' mother accepted the challenge to slide down the pole, she became

James Skinner cottage on Manitou Island, attributed to Cass Gilbert, in 1997

stuck, and neighbors had to be called in to effect a rescue.[22]

In a second commission, the Jasper Tarbox cottage, Gilbert went the opposite direction, toward planar surfaces, playful asymmetries, and roofs that seemed so light that a wind could carry them off. Though documentation is scant, Gilbert has also been credited with the design of a shingled cottage for Tracy Lyon, Tarbox and Morton's neighbor to the north; and the two cottagers beyond Lyon, R. B. C. Bement and E. W. Peet, were also Gilbert clients in St. Paul. If all hired Gilbert at Manitou Island, he ended up doing five consecutive cottages on the northeast shore. Unfortunately, both the Bement and Peet cottages burnt down or were demolished before study of Gilbert's career became of serious interest.[23]

The short southeast bank of the island remained bare until 1892, by which time the Shingle Style had become passé. St. Paul hardware wholesaler William B. Dean, who had already held his property for ten years, was the first to build. Once again, Gilbert was the architect. His manorial colonial revival cottage set the style for the large lots of that stretch of shoreline; Johnston's 1899 design for his friend and cousin Charles M. Power on the east point was suffused with Colonial touches, and Edwin Lundie's 1926 design for Frederick E. Weyerhaeuser on the west complemented the Dean house's stateliness with a vivid and nostalgic pictorialism.

Even with its peninsula and islands, the west bank of White Bear Lake could not contain the increasing numbers of St. Paul residents anxious to build their own cottages. Dellwood was the first of several developments to be platted along the Stillwater rail spur as it turned south along the eastern shore. Named for its undulating surface and tree-dotted knolls, the tract straddled the rail line for a mile and a half. "Trained landscape surveyors and artists" were said to have laid out its 250 acres. The lots varied in size from one quarter to five acres, and each had a frontage of one hundred to five hundred feet and a piece of elevated ground suitable for a cottage.[24]

Prime mover of the new development was St. Paul real estate agent and financier

Walter S. Morton cottage, ca. 1892

Jasper B. Tarbox cottage, ca. 1892

lakeside dining room. One observer claimed it to be so close to the water that one could almost catch fish from the window.[25]

Barnum's buildings may have been the visual landmark, but the vortex of Dellwood's social life in its early years was a pair of properties just to the north. Their owners were two twenty-something bachelors with a common love of boating in all forms—and a taste for night life. Plumbing supplier Lucius P. Ordway and photographer Truman W. Ingersoll shared a dock and presumably a number of parties as well. Ingersoll alone was reported to have had "more visitors probably than any one else at the lake," many of whom found their way into his photograph albums.[26]

Ordway and Ingersoll could not have built cottages more divergent in character. Ordway's was nearly square with a low hipped roof, very much in the style of the eating and dancing pavilions of the day. Its one aristocratic indulgence was a Chinese lattice balustrade encircling the building, an artful advance on the standard Adirondack composite of sticks and branches. A few yards away, Ingersoll rode the wave of the

A. Kirby Barnum. He had a social as well as an economic reason for laying out so large a tract at once: to protect the property from "the desecration of the rowdy, shanty-building element, which comes in to ruin so many sweet summer retreats." Once the land was platted, Barnum immediately set an example by hiring the young Cass Gilbert to

design his cottage, following it with a combined hotel and clubhouse. Begun in mid-1883 and finished the following summer, the two monumental buildings reigned over the Dellwood shoreline for a generation. The clubhouse was particularly remarkable for its belvedere, which offered a dramatic vantage point for eyeing most of the lake, and its

A. Kirby Barnum cottage, viewed from the belvedere of the Dellwood Clubhouse, ca. 1895

Birch Lodge, the Truman W. Ingersoll cottage, in 1889

Truman Ingersoll and friends at Birch Lodge in 1889

future, with a log cabin identical in form and fittings to those that would populate countless northern lake resorts in the 1920s. He named it Birch Lodge after the clumps of trees on either side of it.

Beneath the Ingersoll cabin lay its most unusual feature, a wide-entry basement presumably used for boat storage. The assortment of watercraft lining the dock was something of a curiosity itself. Ingersoll was fascinated by traditional Ojibway canoes of birch bark, so he bought one, along with two sailboats, a rowboat, and a duck boat. A steam launch rounded out the collection. Its engine fired by kerosene, Ingersoll's *Mirella* was the midget among the many steam-powered pleasure boats on White Bear Lake and Minnetonka.[27]

Allen H. Stem, a young architect of social and sporting instincts equal to Ingersoll's, began putting his stamp on Dellwood in 1890, about the same time that Gilbert's presence began to be felt on Manitou Island. For a few years Stem was that rarity among Twin Citians, an equal devotee of both the great vacation lakes. He built his first summer cottage a stone's throw away from the Lafayette Hotel on the north shore of Minnetonka Beach but chose Dellwood for harboring his yacht. The man of the world and the sportsman were nudged into reconciliation in 1893, with the destruction of Stem's Minnetonka retreat by fire.[28]

In the meantime, Stem had already made a significant architectural mark at White Bear Lake. When H. A. Boardman tired of the cramped quarters and rowdy night life of the west shore in 1890, he turned to Stem to design a spacious cottage for his family at Dellwood. The Boardman cottage was pure Shingle Style, but pure Stem as well. For this and all ensuing Dellwood projects, Stem

H. A. Boardman cottage, ca. 1892

shook off the scholarly historical detailing that encrusted his urban designs. Rather than playing off of the Queen Anne, the colonial revival, or some other current fashion, the Boardman design wrapped its shingle skin around simple, geometrical forms and tucked all the porches under a roof that embraced the entire structure. Stem's own

Dellwood cottage, built thirty years later, adhered to much the same aesthetic. A monumental rectangle veneered with stucco, its historical references were confined to such places as half-hidden column capitals and the parlor fireplace.

In the post-World War I era, Dellwood's last great period of summer house construction,

Allen H. Stem house at Dellwood in 1923

picturesque stone cottages and whitewashed colonial revival estates competed for public favor. C. H. Johnston, Jr., and Edwin Lundie, who excelled in both types, were the favored architects. The one invariable attribute of their late Dellwood work was ostentation, which often worked against the otherwise comfortable quality of the summer house spaces. A writer for *Amateur Golfer and Sportsman*, which kept an eye fixed on the Dellwood area, seemed particularly impressed—or nonplussed—by this fusion of sophistication and simplicity when she ascribed to Johnston's E. N. Saunders house a "subtle livable quality that seems a distinct part of [its] pretentious beauty, a quality that magically transforms a great house into an attractive home."[29]

With the Cottage Park, Manitou Island, and Dellwood associations all up and running, White Bear Lake could cater to cottagers of every taste. Those who wished to follow a clannish sort of social life chose Cottage Park; the reclusive and the nature lovers settled on Manitou Island; and the sports-minded gravitated to Dellwood. All

that was needed to settle into any of these communities was money—not to purchase the land, which was offered cheaply enough, but to build a cottage and maintain a lifestyle emulating the neighboring cottagers.

Below Dellwood but still on the Stillwater spur line lay an expanse of shoreline equal to Dellwood's. In 1881 three thousand acres were bought up by the Wildwood Park Association, ostensibly for platting yet another exclusive development. The association was directed by a group of St. Paul merchants and financiers, among them the ubiquitous C. P. Noyes. But the peninsula that the association actually wished to occupy was no larger than Manitou Island. The rest of the land had been purchased on speculation and as a way of protecting the shoreline north and south of the peninsula from unwanted development.[30]

Shortly after the initial purchase, a two hundred-acre tract was donated to a quasi-religious organization known as the Mahtomedi Assembly. The mission of the Mahtomedi Assembly was to build a Chautauqua of the Northwest. A hotel and tabernacle went

Allen and Lucy Stem in Dellwood in the 1920s

89

Living porch, Edward N. Saunders summer house, in 1932

up at the heart of the tract in 1884, and tents and cottages quickly sprang up on the assembly grounds. Lecturers on scientific and literary topics attracted thousands of listeners and summer sojourners. For a brief time, Wildwood appeared to offer a fourth, intellectual or spiritual alternative to the more earthly pleasures of the other three communities.

Enthusiasm for Chautauqua meetings on White Bear Lake proved to be as erratic as it was for similar efforts at Lake Park on Minnetonka. But the initial surge of interest in the Mahtomedi Assembly's programs opened a crack in the armor of class distinction that had threatened to seal off the lakeshore to all but the wealthy. The Mahtomedi cottagers came for the orations and the spiritual exercises, but remained for the lake breezes and the fish. With the transition to ordinary summer life came a social and economic spectrum of summer cottagers that resembled the town of White Bear more than it did the exclusive summer enclaves around the lake.

A short distance northwest of White Bear, Bald Eagle Lake was also settled by an increasingly diverse summer population.

H. H. Bigelow summer house on the Peninsula, ca. 1925

Deserted Chautauqua assembly hall at Mahtomedi, ca. 1895

Among the first of the St. Paul contingent that sought its quiet shores was Dr. Post, a physician who built a pavilion over a mineral spring at its edge. Another was J. Fletcher Williams, renowned historian of St. Paul and Ramsey County, who built his cottage in 1882. But by the mid-1880s less distinguished folk also began to seek it out as an alternative to the boisterous life of the western White Bear shore.

While Manitou Islanders were erecting their five-thousand-dollar cottages, summer settlers on Bald Eagle Lake spent anywhere from five hundred to two thousand dollars. Rather than crowding into an aggressively platted development as at Mahtomedi, the cottages lay nearly hidden from each other in the woods. Their sense of isolation and withdrawal was unusual for a lake favored by city residents, but it would typify thousands of the cottages of the future on lakes far removed from the Twin Cities.[31]

A cottage on Bald Eagle Lake in the 1890s

WATERING HOLES
IN THE GARDEN OF THE WEST

Surrounded by a growth of large timber, with high banks, and some ten islands in its midst,
Prior Lake combines all the elements of beauty and picturesqueness peculiar to our forest lakes,
and is famed for the inexhaustible supply of fish contained in its waters.

Tourist and Sportsman, June 8, 1878

WHILE MINNETONKA and White Bear were coming into their glory, numerous other Minnesota lakes beckoned. The first to attract large numbers of sportsmen and tourists were within the garland of lakes encircling the Twin Cities; shortly behind came lakes scattered through the prairies to the south and southwest. What they all had in common was proximity to a railway line.

Railroad companies made a concerted effort to set the course of tourism, just as they helped to determine the advance of farming and industry. It was hardly coincidental that the first two lakes to offer competition to Minnetonka and White Bear were Prior

Women sewing and reading at Lake Charlotte, ca. 1905

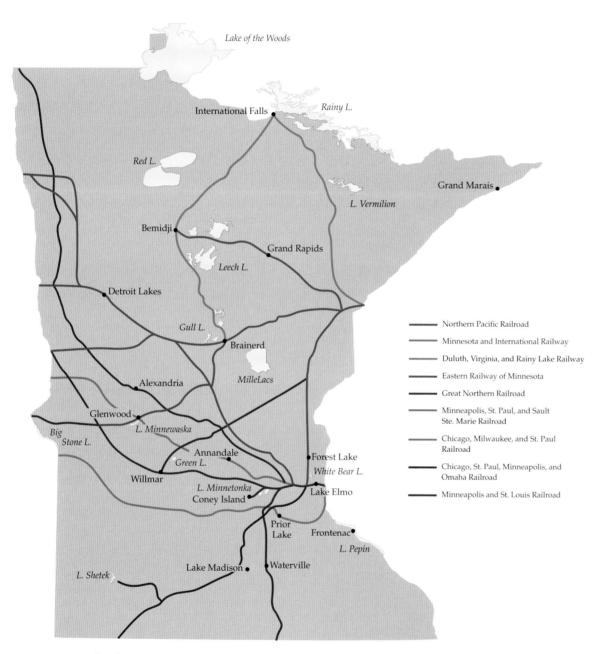

Map legend:
- Northern Pacific Railroad
- Minnesota and International Railway
- Duluth, Virginia, and Rainy Lake Railway
- Eastern Railway of Minnesota
- Great Northern Railroad
- Minneapolis, St. Paul, and Sault Ste. Marie Railroad
- Chicago, Milwaukee, and St. Paul Railroad
- Chicago, St. Paul, Minneapolis, and Omaha Railroad
- Minneapolis and St. Louis Railroad

Map labels: Lake of the Woods, Rainy L., International Falls, Red L., Grand Marais, L. Vermilion, Bemidji, Grand Rapids, Leech L., Detroit Lakes, Gull L., Brainerd, MilleLacs, Alexandria, Glenwood, L. Minnewaska, Big Stone L., Annandale, Green L., Forest Lake, White Bear L., Willmar, L. Minnetonka, Coney Island, Lake Elmo, Prior Lake, Frontenac, L. Pepin, L. Shetek, Lake Madison, Waterville

Main railroad routes to summer cottages in Minnesota in 1910

Lake and Lake Elmo, minor stops on the Chicago, Milwaukee, and St. Paul Railroad (the Milwaukee Road) and the Chicago, St. Paul, Minneapolis, and Omaha Railroad (the Omaha Road), respectively. Both lines cut a swath through the state from east to west, positioning the Twin Cities in the midst of a corridor connecting Chicago and the burgeoning wheat lands of the Northwest.

For a few years in the late 1870s, Prior Lake enjoyed the special patronage of the Milwaukee Road. Named after company superintendent C. H. Prior, its hotel, dining room, and boathouse were run by the local railroad manager, who was also in charge of the town's grain elevators. Milwaukee Road propaganda declared Prior Lake "destined to become a favorite resort, not only for Minneapolis and St. Paul, but the entire Northwest." To help the prophecy along, it hired artist A. M. Shuey to make a sketch of the lake, which it tirelessly pressed into every sort of publication advancing the interests of Minnesota, from the railroad's own *Tourists' Guide of the Northwest* to such

Minnesota-based regional tabloids as *Tourist and Sportsman*, the *Independent Farmer*, and the *Northwest Magazine*. Shuey's drawing captured all the elements that would impel railroad travelers to a Minnesota lake. Wild, high embankments provided a touch of the sublime, three rowboats indicated waters teeming with fish, and a solitary sail bore witness to the leisure opportunities awaiting people of means.

A. S. Dimond of the *Tourist and Sportsman* put in his oar as well. Taking a six A.M. train out of Minneapolis, he journeyed through the outskirts of the vast "Garden of the West," paused at a town appropriately named Farmington, then continued sixty-five cents farther to Prior Lake Station. He found almost nobody in the village and no sign of a lake, but a handcar quickly shot him out to its nearest shore, where he gazed upon its manifold beauties. "It is just one of those places one wants to find," he effused, "when they wish to get away from the busy cares of home and lead a careless, comfortable life, undisturbed by business or people; where one can fish and hunt, and lay around loose,

PRIOR LAKE, MINNESOTA, on the CHICAGO, MILWAUKEE AND ST PAUL RAILWAY.

Artist's view of Prior Lake, first published in 1879

and get plenty of good food, and do just as one likes."[1]

Unfortunately for the future of the resort community, "just as one likes" embraced more than fishing, hunting, and lounging, at least for the increasingly urbane vacationing population of the 1880s. With the emergence of more civilized social activities at Minnetonka and White Bear, Prior Lake slipped

out of the tourism spotlight, and the hotel became just another stop on the line. C. H. Prior himself abandoned ship. In 1883, rather than putting down his summer stakes at his namesake, he built a six-thousand-dollar villa on Expectation Point at Lake Minnetonka. His railroad continued to promote Prior Lake as a fisherman's paradise, but summer settlement along its shores had to

View from Lake Elmo Lodge in 1882

wait nearly fifty years to get much beyond the scattering of cottages built during the lake's moment in the sun.

Like its competitors, the Milwaukee Road also boosted the vacation potential of Minnesota lakes at the furthest remove of the line from the Twin Cites. Big Stone Lake on the Dakota border was a particular target of promotional campaigns. The St. Paul and Pacific Company, which ran a spur to Brown's Valley at the northern end, promoted the lake as well. It was already well known to shippers, as it stood at the head of the Minnesota River and the southern watershed, with the watershed to the north just above it. Numerous fishermen traveled to its long, rocky banks, some of them in large parties. But as at Prior Lake, most stayed at the local hotel or put up tents along the shore. Few committed themselves to land purchase or building of a more permanent sort.[2]

A slightly more successful east-west extreme was promoted by the St. Paul and Sioux City Railroad and an affiliated line to Chicago out of which the Omaha Road was created. Lake Elmo, situated halfway between St. Paul and Stillwater, suddenly ascended in the late 1870s to a "resort of the best classes." Special trains ran out from the city, real estate magnate Peter Berkey built a twenty-thousand-dollar lodge in an ornate Eastlake vein, and throngs of fashionable St. Paulites spent days rowing and sailing on the lake or picnicking and taking carriage drives around it. "Fabulous quantities" of pike and bass leapt from hook to boat during the day, and the evening air was filled with band music and the concussions of bowling pins and billiard balls.

In the early 1880s, the Lake Elmo rage passed as quickly as it had come, and the local press focused on the lake's suddenly quiet beauties. The "foliage embowered gem" evolved into a tranquil retreat for weekenders, and small vacation estates began to dot the shores. Dr. Edward Walther built the best known of these in 1882. His cottage was in fact a simple farmhouse, one side opening to the lake and the other facing large flower and vegetable gardens. Walther's boathouse was a landmark of the lake for many years.[3]

Dr. Edward Walther family at their Lake Elmo cottage in 1890

From St. Paul, the Sioux City division of the Omaha Road wended its way along the Minnesota River, then aimed for the southwestern corner of the state. Not many lakes cropped up along its traverse of the "Great Prairie Garden," but railroad publicists made the most of them. Near the Iowa border, Worthington lay beside a small body of water, and in 1878 a drive was laid out around it. But that and the lakeside railroad park were destined to be enjoyed by few but local residents. A body of water with a brighter future lay to the north near Currie. The Omaha Road built a forty-mile spur to the tiny milling center, and Lake Shetek at its foot became one of the most popular summer retreats in the southern half of the state. Prominent families from the Twin Cities

Henry A. Castle (standing at left) with family and friends at a summer cabin on Lake Shetek in 1897

cottaged on its shores for more than thirty years, but E. F. Drake, the prime mover in the construction of the St. Paul and Sioux City Railroad, was not among them. He sold his interest in the road in 1882 and located his summer house on Manitou Island.[4]

With the completion of its line to Minneapolis and Northome in 1879, the Minneapolis and St. Louis Railroad joined the promotional blitz of Minnesota lakes. Minnetonka was, of course, the ultimate stop for southerners. But the rail line also promoted the watering holes along the way, from Albert Lea in the south ("surrounded by rich and picturesque scenery, ever varied and enchanting") to Lake Tetonka at Waterville and Lake Madison at the edge of the Big Woods. Albert Lea never attracted anything approaching a summer settlement, but Iowa families and fishermen slowly built up the shores of the other two lakes with cottage resorts and private summer houses. As late as 1897, the Minneapolis agent for the railroad advertised the fishing grounds of Tetonka and Madison Lakes to travelers from the north as well as from the South.[5]

Cottage on Lake Madison, ca. 1895

McPeek's Cottages on Lake Tetonka, ca. 1920

At first glance it may seem a bit curious that railroad companies should have promoted near and far lake tourism with equal vigor while paying little attention to so many of the equally scenic lakes in between. They were in fact pursuing two quite different strategies: to expand settlement outward from the Twin Cities and to get travelers to traverse as much available farmland and visit as many town sites as possible on the way to their destination. Seducing them into a remote hotel or out onto a distant lake was the immediate goal of the latter strategy; getting them to resettle somewhere along the railroad line was the ulterior motive.

However well the strategy might have worked for motivating the spread of permanent settlement, it did very little to displace summer cottagers and resorters from their favored haunts around the Twin Cities. At the beginning of 1877, the only resort communities in the state to receive much public notice had been Lake Minnetonka, White Bear Lake, and Frontenac. The tourist bubble of the late 1870s, created in large part by the railroads, put Minnesota summer travelers into hotels and cottages at all the advertised places for a few years, but by the mid-1880s, many were back at Minnetonka and White Bear. Pressure from the railroad companies alone was not enough to disperse the vacationing population away from its favorite Twin Cities area haunts on a lasting basis.[6]

In the meantime, with little promotion from the railroads themselves, numerous summer communities spread out quite naturally along lines branching out from St. Paul and Minneapolis. A division of the Minneapolis, St. Paul, and Sault Ste. Marie Railroad (the Soo Line) traversed Wright County in 1886. From the Annandale or South Haven stops, travelers had twenty-six lakes to chose from, all accessible by road. Resorts catering to fishermen sprang up immediately, with private cottages soon to follow.[7]

According to a long-time Annandale resident, the means of passage from depot to lake infallibly showed the class of the owner. Wealthy summer cottagers kept their own horses on the premises and sent their drivers out on earlier trains to have the carriages ready for them at the station. Fishermen and their families, in the meantime, "were either picked up at the train station by the resort owner or hired a local livery to bring them to their summer lodgings. Carriages transported the passengers, with the luggage following on a dray." Gender distinctions were also not long in asserting themselves. "The men immediately sought out their favorite fishing guide, while their wives and children (if they were fortunate, with a maid in tow) came to a favorite beach or dining table."[8]

A Wright County cottager with particularly conspicuous wealth was St. Paul financier (listed only as "capitalist" in the directories) Daniel N. Dellinger. His pedigreed bay horses made a particularly vivid impression on farmers and villagers when he drove his surrey between town and cottage. The summer place on Cedar Lake was unpretentious enough. Its verandas were scarcely visible from the drive, and the squat belvedere scarcely rose above the lower branches of the trees. But the estate included a guest house, caretaker's cottage, and large stables and

Daniel N. Dellinger cottage on Cedar Lake, ca. 1973

sheds, all a far cry from the fishing cabins of the other summer residents.[9]

Clearwater Lake, the largest body of water in the county, attracted more resort visitors than cottagers, but at least one prominent Minnesotan, Dr. Edward Murray, built a large summer house on the south shore. Murray began his career as a machinist but claimed to have discovered (or developed in his spare hours) a positive cure for alcoholism and other forms of addiction. He established institutions in Minneapolis, Fargo, and Seattle and apparently took a piece of his Minneapolis practice with him to Annandale in the summer. Several rooms of his lake cottage served as a kind of sanitarium, where his patients had the opportunity to dry out in a rural setting. Whether that arrangement succeeded for either his patients or for his family members who occupied the other half of the house has not been told.[10]

Lake Charlotte, reached only by a rather long carriage ride from the Soo Line or the Manitoba Line to the north, developed along a different though equally common track. Anthony Haffner purchased forty acres of

Clara Hatch cottage on Bungalow Beach at Lake Sylvia, ca. 1915

farmland on the north shore in 1889. In spite of its remoteness, the lake attracted numerous tourists, perhaps because its great depth, around a hundred feet, provided unusual fishing opportunities. Many of the fishermen and campers called on Haffner for food, turning his farmhouse into a virtual boarding house. He finally yielded to public demand and gave up farming for a resort business. At first confining his operation to his house, by 1915 he had expanded his venture to ten cottages. His experience

mirrored that of numerous farmers at the west end of Lake Minnetonka and was repeated many times over in other parts of the state where farmers and tourists shared a lake.[11]

An enchanting picture from the turn of the century shows a row of cabins on Lake Charlotte with several women seated in front, each one occupied with sewing or reading. Beneath the pretty image lay a somewhat less charming reality, for these typical feminine pursuits were often simply

Women and boy on lake overlook at Bungalow Beach at Lake Sylvia, ca. 1915

ways of coping with lengthy days in an environment for which long dresses and a distaste for fishing were ill fitted. Perhaps suitably enough, the foremost cabin was named Dolores, meaning one who sorrows.

Many of the small turn-of-the-century resorts in Wright County consisted of little more than clusters of rental cabins with shared facilities such as boat docks and picnic grounds. Bungalow Beach on the north side of Lake Sylvia was a particularly picturesque example. The cabins were built of logs on the first floor, complete with Adirondack style porches, but the gables were framed and shingled, creating a rustic equivalent of a common bungalow type. Just above the beach was a crudely fashioned platform with a boulder fireplace at one end, functioning as a combined belvedere and widow's walk. A picture of the platform in use during the World War I era shows the Lake Charlotte phenomenon brought up to date; the women look hopelessly bored, and a small boy leaning against one of them does not appear to be faring much better.

Carver County to the south of Wright was, to use a nineteenth-century phrase, not as well watered, and its few lakes never managed to compete effectively with Minnetonka. The Minneapolis and St. Louis Railroad connected through to its main resort town, Waconia, the same year as it reached Excelsior, and few tourists thought it worth the extra miles to seek out an assuredly less spectacular—and less sociable—vacation setting. All these caveats aside, however, Lake Waconia, or Clearwater as it was then called, managed one remarkable episode in summer living.

An island in the middle of the lake was purchased in 1884 by Lambert Naegle, manager of the German-language Minneapolis newspaper *Freie Presse*. He used his paper to tout his new property as "The Coney Island of the West," a summer colony "that is created not alone for the rich, but where a poor man can also have his fun for a small amount of money." A just-completed spur of the St. Paul and Pacific Company pushed past the northern end of the lake on its way to Hutchinson, and Coney Island got a depot. Naegle had his place of fun, but it ended up being a bizarre mix of commercial attractions for the working man's family and strangely off-center fiefdoms for the elite.[12]

The half of the island intended for private use went on the market in 1885, and three lots were immediately bought by Minneapolitans of German descent. All were men of wealth. The first, Peter Lindner, immediately opened a drinking establishment, naming it Tivoli after the famed outdoor pleasure gardens in Copenhagen. The business failed to survive two years, but instead of selling off the property, Lindner absorbed it into his private grounds and went into seclusion. His daughter's family named the villa Wacksonia after his death in 1889 and continued to summer there until 1917.

Coney Island's second cottager, John Orth, had established a brewery in St. Anthony in 1851 and from that beginning had grown to be Minneapolis's preeminent beer manufacturer. Orth had already built a three-story summer house on the north shore of the lake. His Coney Island retreat was more intimately scaled but unusually ornate for a northern cottage. The third buyer was Minneapolis physician Henry E. Lutz, who

Joseph and Margarethe Brueck cottage on Coney Island, 1887

107

Emile Amblard at Villa Emile on Coney Island, ca. 1900

built an ordinary enough cottage but installed a patent cyclone shelter beneath it and erected a boathouse significantly larger than the cottage.

These were all minor eccentricities compared to what followed. In 1890 a charismatic Frenchman named Emile Amblard arrived in Waconia. His Gallic flamboyance and romantic past as son of the mayor of Périgueux instantly bedazzled the down-to-earth, agrarian based Germanic population of the town. Reporting on his first visit, the local newspaper announced, "Monsieur E. Amblard of Paris (France) was at the Lake house for several days this week. Magnifique."[13]

The "Duke of Clearwater Lake," as he was soon dubbed, began summering regularly on the island in 1892, probably in the cottage vacated at Orth's death but still owned by his widow. On purchasing the Orth property in 1893, Amblard immediately put in motion an ambitious acquisition, building, and landscaping scheme for the entire west end of the island. All of the horticultural layouts and architectural designs were his own. Two

more cottages went up: Villa Emile, which housed his family, and Villa Topsy (the name of their dog), in which he installed his guests. The original Orth cottage was renamed Villa Marie after his wife and became a retreat for her and her mother.

Though all three cottages were specimens of filigree gone mad, Villa Emile particularly captured the ocean-straddling excesses of its owner. In its general form, a hip-roofed main structure with an engaged square tower, it recalled a type of traditional French country house; but the latticework veranda that wrapped two sides, the patterned shingle roof, and the iron cresting that rode the top of the hips were pure American Victorian, looking more like the follies of the post-Civil War period than the more current exuberance of high Queen Anne fashion. But Amblard had scarcely begun. By the time of his death in 1914, his estate included a boathouse, bath house, five pavilions, and numerous other structures holding, among other things, a billiard room and chess parlor.

A year after Amblard's death, a writer of Carver County's history bemoaned

Waconia's failure to live up to its promise as a resort community. He assigned some of the blame to the "interference" of Minnetonka and some to Coney Island's pattern of exclusive ownership. Amblard had opened some of his gardens to the public in 1913, but it was too little, too late. By World War I, lakeside resorting and cottaging had leapt past Carver County, and all the democratizing in the world would not redeem the island for the new generation of summer cottagers.[14]

On the other side of the Twin Cities, a rail line to Duluth provided very early access to a scattering of lakes along a north-south axis. Neither the St. Paul and Duluth Railroad that built the line nor the Northern Pacific that took it over made any effort to promote stopping anywhere along the route. The lakes along the way were said to be "hemmed in by the forests, making very pretty scenes," but this was a through-the-window description, offered simply as an inducement to take the Duluth Short Line.[15]

Yet a number of distinctive groups of lakes lay along the route, and several proved

Theophil Hummel (second from left) with his family and a friend at the Hummel cottage on Forest Lake, ca. 1910

to be tempting to cottagers. Closest to the Twin Cites and approachable by rail as early as 1866 was a group of lakes about the same distance north of White Bear as that lake is from St. Paul. Chief of these was Forest Lake. Already well established as a fishing and camping site by 1880, it was slow to attract lake visitors willing to erect more permanent structures. At least one small colony of wealthy St. Paul residents arrived at the turn of the century, however. Among them was jeweler Theophil Hummel, whose cottage family tradition assigns to Cass Gilbert. Appearing at first to be a rather ordinary Craftsman bungalow, the design would have suited any number of St. Paul streets—except for a porch at the rear, facing the lake, rather than on the front, facing the road.[16]

North of Forest Lake lies the Chisago Lakes area, a part of the state well-known for its concentration of Scandinavian immigrants. But the lakes themselves, six bays united by straits, remained thinly settled through the nineteenth century, when the banks were still mostly prairie. By the time prominent brewer William Hamm built his

William Hamm cabin on Chisago Lake, ca. 1925

Arnold Schwyzer with his family at their log cabin on Grindstone Lake, ca. 1916

cottage, however, several groves of trees had grown up along many of the shores. Dating to the World War I era, the Hamm cottage drew its materials and design elements from the Craftsman bungalow vocabulary; but the plan responded to its woodland setting in an unusual way. The lake façade stretched out over twice the length of the gable ends, permitting a long, continuous ribbon of windows in front of a combination living room and enclosed porch—sometimes referred to as a "living porch."[17]

Near Sandstone, more than halfway to Duluth along the rail line, is a lake with a particularly colorful summer history. In the mid-1890s, budding St. Paul surgeon Arnold Schwyzer purchased a large tract of land on Grindstone Lake with the intention of joining with friends to convert a major share of the shoreline to recreational use. Schwyzer quickly rose to the top of his profession, and his visions for his vacation property ascended with him. A lakeside pavilion went up in 1896, to be followed by his first summer house and a year-round tenant house in 1900, a "Swiss Chalet" in 1904, a two-story

house addition in 1912, a log cabin in 1919, and a boathouse in 1924.[18]

In addition to the purely recreational buildings were a number of barns and other agricultural structures. Like F. A. Jennings on the West Arm of Lake Minnetonka, Schwyzer ran most of the property as a farm, leaving the day-to-day management and operation to others while he and his family enjoyed themselves. About 250 acres of the 2,500 he eventually acquired on or near Grindstone Lake were under cultivation. The farm's main products were milk and potatoes.

Every third year the Schwyzer family vacationed in Switzerland, where the doctor was born. All the other summers, and numerous long holiday weekends, were spent on the Grindstone Lake farm. When Schwyzer died, the property passed to his children with the adjuration that it remain in the family. But only one child, his daughter Marguerite, remained in Minnesota, and she willed it to its current owners, the Audubon Society.

Compelling fashions often create strange ironies, and the urgency with which Twin

Citians of means boarded trains for lake sites well beyond the city boundaries is certainly among them. While Minnetonka and White Bear Lake swarmed with urban tourists, lakeshores that remained in their pristine state close to the city were almost totally neglected. Their few summer structures of any distinction often enjoyed a sense of wild isolation from the city belied by actual distances. A clubhouse for the Northwestern Kennel Club, arising from the weedy banks of Silver Lake across from North St. Paul, looked for all the world like a gentleman's villa in the midst of the wilderness. It played the part as well, hosting parties of St. Paul's elite in the late 1880s and early 1890s. D. J. Egleston's four-thousand-dollar cottage on Lake McCarron in St. Paul and Charles McC. Reeve's stock farm and summer residence on Lake Harriet in Minneapolis must have presented something of the same wild aspect.[19]

Only Lake Calhoun in Minneapolis had a thriving seasonal colony. Its first summer residents were Minneapolitans of wealth who basked in one of three resort hotels, each built in the late 1870s. The grandest of these, built as the Lake Calhoun Pavilion in 1877 but lavishly outfitted and renamed the Lyndale in 1883, briefly competed with the Lafayette in opulence. When it burned to the ground in 1888, upscale resorting at Calhoun abruptly came to an end.[20]

Cottages and a broader class of summer residents followed in the wake of the hotels, as they had at Minnetonka and White Bear. Louis Menage, owner of two of the hotels, had the foresight to purchase and develop a small plat on the southeast shore of the lake while the resort business was still alive and healthy. Cottage City, as he called it, was laid out in twenty-foot lots, some of them already occupied by tiny seasonal dwellings.

The earliest surviving examples date to 1880 or earlier, but most were constructed in the first decade of the twentieth century.[21]

Summer resorting and cottaging in and around the Twin Cities began to die shortly after World War I for the very reason that it boomed at more distant locations: the arrival of the automobile. It was no longer necessary for vacationers to settle on lakes near railroad stations. The automobile offered the freedom to explore areas that had only recently been reached by rail lines or, in some cases, reached for the first time by automotive roads. At the same time, the convenience that had at first attracted tourists now repelled them, as the railway depots became magnets for year-round populations.

Summer settlements well away from the cities were relatively unscathed by the transition from train to automobile, however. The key point was simply that getting to them required a lengthy drive. As auto tours became fashionable in themselves, traveling a good distance became at least as important as finding an unspoiled spot. As a result, old summer establishments on the Soo Line,

Northwestern Kennel Club clubhouse on Silver Lake, ca. 1900

such as those on Lake Whipple in Pope County and Elbow Lake in Grant County, continued to thrive while their Wright County cousins, whose lakes remained equally unspoiled, wilted.

With the fading of the resort business around the Twin Cities came an indirect benefit for a large part of the vacationing population. Resorts such as those on Lake Pulaski near Buffalo sold off their rental cottages at low cost for use as summer cabins, or they subdivided the land for others to build cottages. This gave families of limited income an easy means of owning what still looked and felt like vacation property— at least until the town's population crept around the lake to engulf them. Similar circumstances had created identical opportunities in Mahtomedi on White Bear Lake in the late 1880s, but now the phenomenon spread to lakes in a wide arc west and north of the cities.[22]

Relaxing by a cabin on the south shore of Lake Calhoun, ca. 1905

LAKES WITHOUT NUMBER

*One should make a vacation trip to the Lake Park region of Minnesota
because it is a place of beauty, of health, of joyous outdoor life. Its lofty hills,
graceful slopes, verdant nooks, crystal streams, limpid lakes, innumerable pleasure resorts,
boating, fishing, outdoor sports, will make you stronger, purer, and nobler.*

Minnesota Lakes, 1906

THE WESTERN CRESCENT

Between 1871 and 1890, three railroads pushed northwest out of St. Paul and Minneapolis to the plains of North Dakota and Manitoba. By a sheer coincidence of geography,
the tracks overlay a wide arc of dense lakeland running west from the Twin Cities to
Kandiyohi County, then curving north through Glenwood, Alexandria, and Detroit
Lakes (then called simply Detroit) before hooking northeast to Bemidji. Transportation

Ernest Oberholtzer cabin on Mallard Island, Rainy Lake, ca. 1950

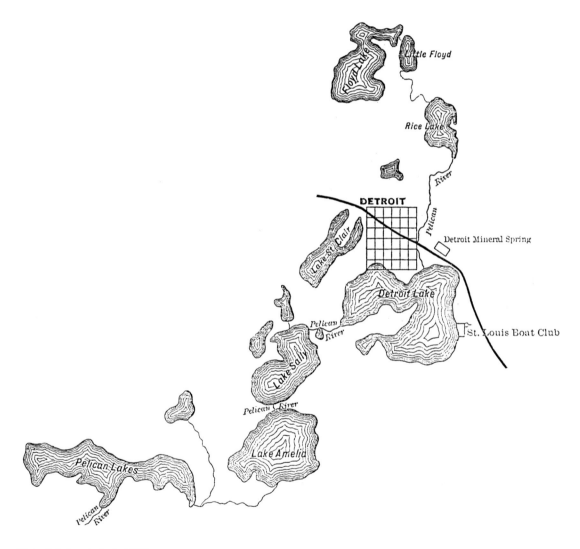

Detroit Lakes chain in 1900

routes created to push people and supplies westward evolved into the state's first major recreation corridor.

Trainloads of tourists camped, cottaged, and stayed at resorts on lakes in this grand, wild parkland for a full generation before the arrival of the automobile. First the Northern Pacific, then the Manitoba Road, and finally the Soo Line vied for their patronage. The romantic designation "Lake Park Region" was probably coined by the railroads themselves. Each put different boundaries around the region, depending on the route of its particular tracks. All sang the praises of distant resort towns and lakes with the same glowingly vague terms that immigration officials used to promote Minnesota as a whole. The water was sapphire, the forests emerald, the sky as blue as Italy's, the fish population inexhaustible, and the piney, ozone-laden air a natural cure for most of what ailed the human species.[1]

Railroad travel through the western crescent of the lake region was possible by 1871. But tourism, at least the sort of summer travel that regularly displaced people from their homes for much of the season, had not yet arrived. As late as 1878, the best that could be said of Minnesota's Lake Park Region was that dozens of sites along the Northern Pacific and St. Paul and Pacific routes were "destined to be grand resorts in the near future, if the people would but try to make them such."[2]

The pivotal year for the Lake Park Region was 1879, as it was for its gateway lake west of the Twin Cities. That was the year that both the Harrow (soon to be the St. Louis) and the Lake Park Hotels on Minnetonka opened to great fanfare. It also marked the reorganization of the troubled St. Paul and Pacific Company into the aggressive St. Paul, Minneapolis, and Manitoba Railway and the completion of a new main route as far as Fergus Falls. The indefatigable James J. Hill was about to get into the tourism business. In the meantime, the older Northern Pacific line had succeeded in connecting St. Paul to its eventual transcontinental line at Moorhead in 1877 and was gearing up for tourism as well.

Detroit, nine-tenths of the way to Moorhead on the Northern Pacific line from St. Paul, was the first northern town to develop a substantial summer community. It had been settled by the Boston Colony, a group of former volunteer soldiers from New England who wanted to "grow up with the country." They first planned on settling in Kansas, but their leader, Colonel George Johnson, persuaded them to avoid the "scorched and malarial" South and seek out lands along the Northern Pacific route. In 1870 Johnson explored the route through northern Minnesota with the president of the company, ultimately settling on the township that the New Englanders would purchase.[3]

The town Johnson's colony platted lay on a large lake that, as it happened, possessed a mineral spring. That was enough to initiate a small tourism industry. A contingent of St. Louis sportsmen joined with Minnesotans to form the Detroit Lake, St. Louis, St. Paul and Minneapolis Fishing and Shooting Club in 1879. So began one of the first, if not the first, of the many interstate outing associations that would crop up on the shores of Minnesota lakes over the next fifty years. The St. Louis Club, as locals called it, imme- diately built a clubhouse and the rudiments of a cottage community.

A first class resort hotel, the Minnesota House, went up with eastern money in 1880, and Detroit began to draw all three types of Minnesota tourists: pleasure seekers, sports- men, and invalids. The lake margin closest to town was platted in cottage lots, inviting both tourists and townspeople to establish private summer retreats. But the county had more than two hundred other lakes as well, nine of them linked to Detroit Lake in a chain extending forty miles from north to south.[4]

In an effort to exploit outlying lake attractions, lumber merchant John K. West organized the Detroit Lakes and Pelican Valley Navigation Company. Formed in 1888, the company proposed to turn the Detroit Lake chain into a national tourist attraction. They had their work cut out for them. All that tied the chain together was the Pelican River, a narrow, meandering stream of variable depth; the lakes were also at sev- eral different levels. West's company tackled the problem by carving out an elaborate

J. W. Smith cottage on Detroit Lake, ca. 1895

system of channels and dams, which opened the lower four lakes to steamboat traffic and lengthened the shoreline available to cottagers to nearly two hundred miles. This was an extraordinary enterprise for its day, a waterway engineering project with no natural resources to exploit, no distant town to settle, no farmland to open up, no linkage to some other transportation conduit. Its sole commercial purpose was summer tourism.

But West's novel venture proved itself many times over. For twenty years beginning in 1889, a steamboat traversed the route

through the chain of lakes three times a day, carrying sightseers and summer cottagers. The Northern Pacific delivered tourists from points east and south, as expected, but it also brought in a succession of North Dakotan and Canadian summer residents. By 1896 seventy-five cottages had been built, and plans were under way for that many more. Like Excelsior in the 1880s, the town at the center of the chain evolved into a community of seasonal service-related industries. A local saying was born, that Detroiters "lived on fish and strangers."[5]

Most of the cottagers along the connected lakes built in the humble fashion dictated by their reliance on water transport for building materials. But the summer houses of the Detroit Lakers, especially those staying close to the town, vied with the ostentation of the turn-of-the-century Minnetonka mansions. The dominant mode was colonial revival in Shingle Style dress, as it had been at White Bear Lake ten years earlier. A raised, lake boulder foundation became the signature of the town's elite, and the finest homes were John K. West's, Oakenwald, and the Stoneycroft estate of Elon and Lucy Holmes.

Elon G. Holmes was Detroit's most distinguished and best-loved citizen. He had followed the progress of the Northern Pacific Railroad to the town in 1871 to set up the first store and open the first bank. Nine years later he financed the town's opera block, before serving terms as county commissioner and state senator. Stoneycroft was built when "Uncle Elon," as the townsfolk called him, neared his sixtieth birthday; he probably intended to use it as a retirement home after his business career wound down. The

Stoneycroft, the Elon G. Holmes cottage on Detroit Lake, in 1972

Holmses had three servants to help manage the cottage and the active social life in which it surely played a prominent role.[6]

Detroit's success as a resort spurred the Northern Pacific Railroad to promote tourism elsewhere along the line. Company president Thomas H. Canfield was particularly keen on pulling water-starved North Dakotans into the state. He envisioned Lake Cormorant, the westernmost lake of any size in the region, as "the great summer resort in the future," an honor he was willing to divide with Lake Minnetonka.

Distance from an established population center kept Canfield's prophecy in the realm of fantasy. Tourism could not create towns; it could not even establish a foothold without a thriving local economy. The economic base could be lumber, as it was in Detroit, but it could also be farming. On its way to North Dakota, the Northern Pacific route sent out numerous feeder lines to grain storage and milling centers, and the most enterprising of these towns promoted the beauty and piscine riches of its lakes as much as the fertility of its farmland.

Lake Whipple catapulted into public attention when a tentacle of the Northern Pacific passed its adjacent town of Glenwood in 1878. Lined with picturesque coves and inlets and surrounded by rolling terrain, Whipple's extraordinary scenic values had been noted by Whitefield twenty years earlier. "The true and original White Bear Lake," he declared—for that was its first name— "is five or six times as large as the Ramsey County one, and ten times more beautiful." Once the railroad line was in place, Twin Citians flocked out to sightsee and fish. By the mid-1880s, when the lake received its third name, Minnewaska, cottages began to appear among the trees. Connections to the Manitoba Road and Soo Line brought in additional waves of tourists. By 1900 cottagers from as far away as Omaha and Chicago mixed with the Minnesotans. All lived in small frame retreats, partly hidden from both water and neighbor by the dense woods.[7]

Park Rapids, a wheat-farming center at the top of the western crescent nearly imitated Detroit's ploy. Thirty-five miles north of the Northern Pacific line, the town's lead-

ing businessmen and financiers formed their own railroad company in 1891 to build a spur to Wadena Junction. Soon outgoing grain was met by incoming tourists, thanks to a set of three manually operated locks allowing boaters to negotiate the twenty-one-foot difference in levels between area lakes. Increased lake access meant the creation of a succession of small resorts and the arrival of a flurry of cottagers.[8]

Numerous lake communities and villages on and near the Manitoba Road vied with the popular Northern Pacific stops in the 1880s. Control of commercial traffic across the northern tier of states and into Canada remained the railroad's primary goal, but under Hill's leadership, the company also encouraged summer retreats to lakeside towns along the way. A succession of lakes in Douglas County and Green Lake in Kandiyohi County were particular early favorites among fishermen, giving rise to summer settlements of quite a different character.

Douglas County was reported to have more water surface than land, and its county

A modern cabin near Park Rapids, ca. 1957

seat, Alexandria, lay at the base of a chain of six picturesque lakes: Rowley, Le Homme Dieu, Carlos, Darling, Miltona, and Ida. All but Le Homme Dieu were named after Douglas County pioneers. A few miles to the east on the Manitoba Road, a single large lake with equal scenic beauty, Osakis, straddled the Douglas-Todd County line.

Several small hunting and fishing resorts near Alexandria area made the area's first concerted pitch to railway tourists. The railroad cooperated by offering excursion discounts to both the Osakis and the Alexandria stops and granting greater reductions to small parties. Only the limited number of local accommodations held tourism in check. A remedy came in 1883 with the opening of Hotel Alexandria. Heralded as "one of the leading events in Minnesota summer resort history," it led to a wealthy, varied, and far-flung clientele at least matching that of the Minnesota House in Detroit. Like the St. Louis and Lafayette Hotels on Lake Minnetonka, Hotel Alexandria would also be a catalyst for extensive lot purchase and private cottage construction.[9]

Alexandria's nearest lake, Rowley, was rechristened Lake Geneva, after the famed Swiss resort area, and the shores of Geneva, Le Homme Dieu, Carlos, and Darling all filled with cottages over the next forty years. The Wild Haven Club, an outing organization of St. Paul families, located on a triangle between Lakes Carlos, Darling, and Le Homme Dieu. But Miltona, the northernmost of the group, was destined for primacy among the lakes. Three wealthy outing clubs settled on Miltona in the early 1890s: the Chicago Club; the Minnesouri Club, made up of Minneapolis and Kansas City people; and the Monmouth Club, composed of residents from that Illinois town.

Each of the outing clubs functioned much the same way as the exclusive associations at White Bear and Minnetonka. Members built cottages costing from five hundred to three thousand dollars, danced and listened to music in lakeside pavilions, dined in the clubhouse, and boated on launches or sailboats. The annual Chicago Club regatta was one of the highpoints of the lake's summer life. Fishing was, however, still the primary

A cottage or clubhouse, probably belonging to one of the outing clubs, on a lake near Alexandria, ca. 1895

recreation, at least during daylight hours. Women and children often joined in, but there were also enough of them present at each club for them to organize their own activities.[10]

The Minnesouri Club had a particularly rich history. Incorporated in 1890, its express purpose was "instruction and mutual improvement in the art of angling, [and] the social culture and entertainment of its members." Meals and meetings took place in a hodgepodge structure constructed from pieces of another building hauled to the site. This was all the unpretentious Minnesourians would ever have for a clubhouse. During the first generation of ownership, all sporting activity stopped on Sunday. When evening arrived, club members were shep-

herded into the dance pavilion on top of the boathouse for an hour-long song service.[11]

Green Lake accommodated quite a different sort of summer settlement. The largest and roundest of Edwin Whitefield's beloved Kandiyohi lakes, it lacked the picturesque irregularities in shoreline and terrain that brought distant travelers to Lake Whipple and the Alexandria chain. Fishermen sought it out for the great depth of its waters, its freedom from reeds and rushes, and the sense of privacy created by an encirclement of woods. Its typical cottagers have always been Minnesotans, bunched in settlements close to the shore. The cottages were built for a single purpose: to provide a roof for those rare hours not spent out on the lake.[12]

Had it not been for the enterprise of a single individual, Green Lake would have remained largely inaccessible through Minnesota's first great period of outstate tourism. In 1882 it still lay isolated between the old Breckenridge division of the Manitoba Road and the new, more northerly route through St. Cloud. But Willmar merchant, banker, and developer John Spicer saw the widespread economic advantages of a line that would connect southwest agricultural land to the port facilities of Duluth, intersecting the two northwestern-reaching railroads. Naturally, the line he envisioned would run through Willmar itself. He and several other investors formed the Lake Superior, Willmar and Dakota Railroad Company and, with the backing of James J. Hill, completed the Willmar-to-St. Cloud segment in 1886.

Green Lake lay hidden behind a thin wall of trees next to the new line, and a town instantly sprang up on its western bank. Named after Spicer by Hill himself, it served the growing tourist traffic to the now easily accessed south shore of the lake. During the peak years of the 1880s and 1890s, excursion trains

Medayto, the John Spicer lake cottage and farmhouse on Green Lake, ca. 1895

ran to Spicer from Willmar, Sioux City, Sioux Falls, St. Cloud, and the Twin Cities, bringing a steady stream of resorters and cottagers.

John Spicer, who had started it all, purchased three-quarters of a mile of lakeshore from the Manitoba Road while the rail line was still under construction, adding agriculture to his many ventures. By 1893 the Green Lake farm had become his primary interest, and he began to build a "cottage" that towered over those to the west. He named both farm and farmhouse-cottage Medayto, the Dakota equivalent of Green Lake.[13]

Medayto was a castle among cottages, a soaring Victorian pile of gables and towers. Following the pattern established at Manitou Island at White Bear Lake, dining, living, and sitting rooms occupied the main floor,

with bedrooms above and a kitchen installed in the basement. First- and second-story verandas presented splendid lake vistas, but family and friends often gathered to view sunsets on a broad, two-tiered stairway between the shore and the house. According to oral tradition, rocks piled on either side of the steps absorbed enough heat during the day to keep mosquitoes from descending as darkness approached.

A complete remodeling of Medayto Cottage in 1913—said to be inspired by John and his son Jessie's trip to England—stripped it of both Victorian playfulness and summer character. But the same year brought a new generation of cottagers to the lake. Their favored stretch of lakeshore, known as Crescent Beach, was settled slowly and sporadically until the statewide surge in summer cabin building of the 1950s.[14]

The Black cottage at Crescent Beach on Green Lake in 1915

Gateway to the summer estate of H. H. Broach on Sibley Lake in 1979

THE NORTH WOODS

Near the top of the Lake Park Region's western crescent is a triangular cluster of lakes in the heart of the North Woods. Though every bit as well-supplied with water and fish as its counterpart to the west, it lagged a generation behind as a draw for summer vacationers. This part of Minnesota lay well outside the major corridors of agricultural expansion. Railroads did not pierce it until the late 1890s, and when they arrived, their business was to move lumber, not a pioneering population. Such summer homes as there were clustered around a handful of lakes within easy reach of railroad towns or were built by local people for their own use. The latter, especially in the Leech Lake area, often occupied land denuded of all its marketable timber.[15]

Without the automobile, that situation might have been perpetuated indefinitely. In the initial fury to strip the forests of their marketable timber, the railroad companies extended little encouragement or accommodation to tourists. Until the timber resources were depleted, a large and mobile population at the lakes would have been a detriment to logging had it been possible at all. Yet the railroads established towns and built hotels, unintentionally forming the skeletal structure of another great touring corridor of the future.

As the diminution of logging operations opened up the lakes for sportsmen and wilderness lovers, the Northern Pacific touted the region north of Brainerd as "the cream of the Minnesota climate, lakes, and prairies." Its principal attraction was said to be its primeval character. "Here nature is nature, unadorned, soothing, restful, wooing, unconventional, and unartificial. It means that the man living in Chicago may, if he desires, jump from the twentieth century back into the eighteenth."[16]

Brainerd was already a highly visible stop on the railroad. Since the early 1880s, it had been the heart of the Northern Pacific operation in Minnesota. The major repair shops

A cottage in scrub growth at Leech Lake, ca. 1915

Nellie Whitcomb at her easel at Pelican Lake, ca. 1902

were there and, just as importantly, the railroad company's hospital and sanitarium. When regular tourism began to develop on other railroad lines west and south of Brainerd, the town tentatively began to promote itself as the gateway to the northern forests. Small hotels were built on the banks of Gull Lake to the west and Serpent Lake to the east. By 1887, with the help of rural residents, seventy overnight guests could be accommodated locally, still a tiny number compared to the capacity of the grand hotels at Detroit Lakes and Alexandria.[17]

The summer cottagers who usually followed in the wake of the resorts were slow in coming, in part because the resorts themselves lacked the size or appeal to attract men wealthy enough to create their own summer niche. A push from the railroad itself finally got the process underway. In the 1890s the Northern Pacific began to sell off large tracts of land to colonizing agencies and individuals. James M. Elder, a native of Kentucky, bought out a realty company that had purchased forty thousand acres of railroad land. The land agency he organized would, more than any other single force, put the Brainerd area squarely on the tourist map.

Under Elder's management, the Minnesota Park Region Land Company placed hundreds of sportsmen and sportsmen's associations on the lakes around Brainerd. Among the best known of these was a group of fishermen from Lincoln, Nebraska, known as the Pelican Lake Outing Club. Incorporated in 1902, the PLOC bought 101 acres of Pelican Lake beachfront for $7.50 an acre. The sole woman among the sixteen charter members, Nellie Whitcomb, was invited aboard to act as secretary. She was also the only member of the group not drawn to the North Woods by bass and muskies; her love was painting, at which she was said to be quite accomplished.[18]

For their clubhouse, the PLOC put up a twenty-by-thirty-foot structure of rough logs with porches on two sides and a plain board seat along the other two. The cabins that followed were of equally crude construction. Corrugated iron often served for roofing. Every second lot was reserved for club ownership, creating wide breathing room between cabins. Cutting live timber was strictly prohibited except under direction of the club.

In the early years, club members brought a cook with them to provide meals to the men who came alone. But an increasing number of PLOC members brought their families with them. Several nonmember families also purchased land on the club tract and built their own cabins, paying an annual rent to the corporation.

The experiences of the E. R. Mockett family of Lincoln typified the many trials of establishing a summer retreat in so primitive a setting. Traveling by train to the tiny stop of Smiley, they were met by wagons that took them to the Pelican Lake camp. After a wagon breakdown, they arrived on the site just in time to pitch their tent, shovel sand on the canvas at the bottom of the tent, and hang mosquito netting over the front opening.

After two weeks, the Mocketts decided to build a log house for the next year, buying the logs as standing trees from a farmer across the lake. After cutting them down and hauling them to the lakeshore, they formed them into a boom to be dragged through shallow water by horses to a bay from which a rowboat tugged them to camp. The logs were then pulled up one at a time by horses and laid up into the cabin walls. Mockett ended his account of the first summer's stresses with the assurance that "Mrs. Mockett thinks this country good for her health."[19]

E. R. Mockett family and their newly completed log cabin at Pelican Lake in 1904

Simple cabins and lodges remained the rule as other Brainerd area lakes opened to summer settlement. The Pines on Lake Hubert was typical of the flurry of house and resort building in the first two decades of the new century. Its founder, a Mrs. Osborn, arrived by train and wagon in 1901. She and her son lived in a crude, squared-log shack built by a neighbor while their house was under construction. But even the finished house was a strange hodgepodge of log and frame construction, lacking both the artful craftsmanship of the traditional log cabin and the eye-catching appeal of a well-planned bungalow. Mrs. Osborn added a number of summer cabins to her lodge in 1913, but these had an even more makeshift air about them.[20]

An enormous transformation of the Brainerd area lakes—and of cabin settlements at popular summer sites everywhere—took place in the years following World War I. Up to this point, the traditional log cabin was largely an expedient for summer builders, the result of a willing and sometimes enthusiastic embrace of the strictures of life in the wilder-

The Osborn cottage and log cabin near Lake Hubert, ca. 1915

ness. Its most prized aesthetic qualities bordered on the accidental, born as much of the nature of logs themselves and the structural requirements of forming them into a house as of conscious choices or allegiance to a tradition. But just before World War I, numerous architects began to be interested in the log cabin, and by the 1920s, it had become high art. The accidental and vernacular sources of its visual appeal gave way to a painstaking control of the materials and an assertion of period tastes.

Pelican Lake did not long remain in the hands of wilderness purists and primitivists.

Shortly after World War I, Minneapolis publisher and avid sportsman Wilford H. Fawcett purchased the point above the PLOC camp and immediately set about building a resort that would be a benchmark of the good life on the lakes for years to come. Breezy Point's farmhouse and handful of broken-down cottages gave way to a lavish resort employing more than a hundred employees. The main lodge was Fawcett's particular plaything. Its spacious dining facility, elegantly furnished rooms, gigantic fireplaces, and above all, casino gambling operation pulled a worldwide cast of movie

Gable end of the Wilford H. Fawcett cabin in 1979

Living room of the Fawcett cabin in 1979

stars and other celebrities into an aggressively stylized woodland environment.[21]

The lodge has been gone for nearly forty years, but Fawcett's summer house on the grounds remains an emblem of the log cabin's sudden emergence in the world of architectural fashion. In the hands of Minneapolis architects Magney and Tusler, geometries latent in traditional construction, such as projecting log corners and exposed trusses, became focal points of the design.

Shawano, the H. H. Broach cabin on Sibley Lake, in 1979

All logs were selected for absolute straightness, carefully stripped, and cut to form smooth and perfectly perpendicular ends.[22]

Quite a different but equally pretentious log cabin went up on Sibley Lake a few miles to the west. A stone's throw from both road and rail line, the H. H. Broach cabin of 1926–27 displayed considerably more freedom in the selection and shaping of materials than did the Fawcett cabin. A long wall and gateway mixing boulders and cobblestones introduced the estate. The driveway entered the property under a high arch in which the cobblestones were arranged to spell out "Shawano" in large letters.

Broach headed the International Brotherhood of Electrical Workers, a Chicago-based trade union. As one might guess from the magisterial approach and sheer scale of the summer estate, he was no believer in distributed power. In fact his strong-armed tactics and personal use of union funds led to a widely publicized lawsuit brought by electrical workers in 1932. Among his peccadilloes may have been his dipping into the Electrical Workers Benefit Association fund for the mortgage that financed Shawano.[23]

Gull Lake ultimately became the most prestigious address in the Brainerd area, second only, on a statewide basis, to Minnetonka. But until the 1920s, no one could have predicted its meteoric rise among the state's resort lakes. The railroad made a wide hook to the east just above Brainerd, postponing removal of the lakeshore's last stand of timber until 1911. By that time an automotive

Lake development. The same material, this time in a decoratively knotty grade, carried through to the wall and ceiling paneling of the interiors. Cabins like this were built by the scores in the 1930s, showing that many vacationers had discretionary income not touched by the economic woes saddling most of their compatriots.[25]

Floyd B. Olson cabin on Gull Lake at the start of demolition in 1990

road ran directly by the lake, the only significant deviation of the route north of Brainerd from the original rail corridor. James Elder led the way at Gull Lake as he had at Pelican, establishing a colony of cottagers who built in the typical small-scale, haphazardly designed fashion. But these few fishermen's cabins formed the basis of the Gull Lake Recreational Area, which by 1960 embraced ten thousand summer inhabitants.[24]

Among Gull Lake's best-known seasonal residents were three governors: Floyd B. Olson, Luther Youngdahl, and C. Elmer Anderson. Governor Olson's house of 1933

was particularly noteworthy, a splendid plank and boulder structure that epitomized the faux-rustic tastes of Depression-era builders and artisans. The first floor was covered in split-faced granite rubble carefully laid to make both fitting and color distribution appear utterly (and deceitfully) random. A fireplace of the same material stood at the end of a single-story wing known as the "great hall." Pine tongue-in-groove boards sheathed the second floor of the adjoining kitchen and bedroom wing, which was a reworking of a structure possibly dating to the 1915 beginnings of intensive Gull

Great hall of the Floyd B. Olson cabin in 1990

Rest Cottage nearing completion near Garfield Lake in Cass County, ca. 1910

Lakes at the northwestern extreme of the Lake Park Region, where the crescent and triangle join, opened to tourism in the same laggard way as Gull Lake—and for much the same reason. The first railroad reached Bemidji in 1899, and it took another fifteen years for logging companies to strip the area of its prime timber resources. But in the meantime, conservation concerns about remaining forestlands had led to the creation of a vast publicly managed forest domain in 1902. First named the Minnesota National Forest, then the Chippewa National Forest, the tract included much of the northern lake region served by the Minnesota and International Railway.[26]

Public ownership at first barred settlement on the lakes that fell within the national forest. But in 1909 Cass Lake resident Frank Gorenflo received a permit to build a cottage on Star Island in the middle of Cass Lake. Gorenflo's purpose was a limited one, to isolate his wife and children from the tuberculosis sufferers who frequented the Cass Lake area, but his permit opened the way to one of the densest and most active enclaves of summer settlement in the North Woods.

The U.S. Forest Service set aside all the shoreline of Star Island, the east shore of Cass Lake, and most of the shore line of Pike Bay, its southern extension, for summer cottages. The property was divided into 150-foot lots leased at fifteen dollars a year. By 1920 a number of Cass Lake businessmen and two outing clubs (including one for Minneapolis girls) had chosen sites on the south shore of the island. They were joined by six families from Kansas City, Missouri, and Lincoln, Nebraska, who came north to escape the heat.[27]

What made the island particularly compelling for summer residents was its virgin stand of red and white pine that had somehow escaped the lumberman's ax. Cottagers banded together in 1916 to form the Star Island Protective League, which fought commercial encroachment, including the building of a bridge from the mainland, for more than thirty years. The east and west banks filled with cottages in the 1920s, many of them owned by University of Minnesota professors.

Nearly all of the cabins were simple log or board-and-batten structures more in keeping with cottaging standards at remote, pre-World War I lake sites than with modern fashions or conveniences. Their only touch of luxury was a massive native stone or brick fireplace. Names were an indication of how irreverently these doctors, professors, and businessmen regarded their summer homes. Rather than gracing them with Indian or English-style labels like Shawano or Stoneycroft, they called them Addmore, Little Red Hen, Pioneer, and Fallen Pine. Forest Service officer W. L. Dutton declared them "unattractive and out of keeping with advanced ideas of summer home architecture."[28]

One Star Island cottager, however, insisted on making a unique statement. In the mid-1920s, William King erected a three-story pagoda. As stunning in the snow as it was among trees in leaf, its ground floor opened broadly to the site through a large arch with a gatelike door. Several boathouses and beach houses were built in this fashion in the 1920s, but this was the only Minnesota pagoda designed for long-term human occupancy.

William King cottage on Star Island, Cass Lake, ca. 1950

Cass Lake residents vigorously promoted the unique natural resources of their area even as they fought off development by local entrepreneurs. As early as 1909, the *Cass Lake Times* touted Star Island, crudely settled as it then was, as a perfect summer home for President William Howard Taft. In the late 1920s, when summer home living among the wealthy had become an extension of suburban life, the Cass Lake Commercial Club invited President Coolidge to make use of the Pennington Estate on the shore of the lake. However, neither the tall pines, the telephone connections, nor the proximity to a golf course seduced either president to the wilds of the Northwest.[29]

During the first great flurry of summer migration to the North Woods, resort and cabin builders failed to penetrate much farther east than the Brainerd-Bemidji axis, though railroads and lumbering roads provided easy access to hundreds of additional lakes. The one notable exception was a stretch of the Northern Pacific route (and road to follow) connecting Brainerd and Duluth. The lumbering centers of Aitkin and

McGregor became favorite tourist destinations not long after the turn of the century, with rough-and-ready resorts and cabins soon following.

Rice Lake north of McGregor, under the new and more romantic moniker of Minnewawa, followed a typical course. Dr. D. W. Sherraden and U.S. Marshall William Warner, both of Omaha, put up log-and-boulder cottages around 1910, and two years later a Minneapolis real estate agent bought several hundred acres on a peninsula projecting into the center of the lake. Promoting it as "the most picturesque spot in all Minnesota," the land agent platted it into 596 lots of one-fourth to one acre and marketed them for sporting lodges or family cottages, offering to erect log cabins on the installment plan.[30]

The Grand Rapids area was much more typical of eastern stretches of the North Woods. Early cabin builders came not from the Twin Cities, let alone Chicago or Omaha, but from the area itself. Some were bachelor farmers who banded together in informal outing clubs; others were rural families whose land included low-lying lakeshore

D. W. Sherraden and William Warner cabins on Lake Minnewawa, ca. 1913

property of marginal agricultural value. First generation Finns had a particular affinity for summer cottages on barren shores, perhaps echoing the summer villas of their childhoods. They could be of logs with traditional dovetailed corners or of frame construction sheathed in hand-split shakes; small size and manual fabrication of nearly all building components were the only constants.[31]

Among the earliest resorts in the Grand Rapids area was a lodge built by Erve Martin on Trout Lake, "tucked under the protecting arm of the hills." Following the pattern of countless small resorts everywhere in the state, the main building was also the summer house of the owners, who offered up its largest room for dining and other social gatherings. The Martin lodge went up in

Irve Martin and his family and friends at the Martin Cabin on Trout Lake, ca. 1907

1904, nearly a decade before log cabin construction became high fashion. After a disastrous fire in 1906, it was rebuilt with a large porch and an attic window turned on its corner to look like a diamond. It was only a stock sash, however, its slightly rectangular shape creating the same effect of naïve artifice with materials at hand as the crude embellishments of the Finnish cabins.[32]

Trout Lake repeated the story of Pelican Lake, for the rough artistry of the Martin Resort was soon complemented by a recreational complex that was as costly and self-consciously artistic as the Martin place was

Finnish bachelor Oscar Pelander and friends at his cabin on Balsam Lake, ca. 1905

economical and primitive. By 1915 the prime forest land in the Grand Rapids area had been cut over, leaving only scattered, secluded areas with large tracts of standing timber. One such area was a peninsula jutting from the west shore of Trout Lake. David Joyce, scion of an Iowa lumber baron who had helped found the Itasca Lumber Company, purchased the peninsula in 1915 and began construction of his grandiose summer estate two years later.

Joyce's dream was a compound fashioned after the great camps of the Adirondacks in the late nineteenth century but with all the conveniences and recreational opportunities of a modern suburban estate. By 1921, he had finished fifteen buildings, each constructed of peeled, sanded, and varnished logs. The main lodge, cabins for domestic staff and guests, and caretaker's complex had fireplaces, running water, and electric lights. A telephone system with eleven thousand feet of wire fed into the Grand Rapids exchange, and he kept ready a fleet of power boats and a seaplane.[33]

Dubbed Nopeming, Ojibway for "place of rest," the Joyce estate did everything possible to fulfill its name. A golf course, tennis court, and greenhouse were added to the complex in the 1920s. For more passive relaxation, guests could sit in a woodland pergola overlooking the main lodge and the lake. This observatory was among the showiest, and certainly the most romantic, pieces of Adirondack construction in Minnesota. Its direct inspiration was not the woods themselves but nostalgia for an era of faux-wilderness extravagance that had come and gone thirty years before.

Predominantly local summer settlement on lakes east of the Brainerd-Bemidji axis rapidly changed with the coming of the

Observatory at Nopeming, the David Joyce summer estate on Trout Lake, in 1980

automobile. A cottaging boom overtook the lakes north of Grand Rapids in the late 1920s, with the town of Marcell at the center. A St. Paul newspaper reported that in 1926 a single lodge owner disposed of lots to three men from Chicago, four from Minneapolis, four from St. Paul, two from Mankato, one from Oklahoma, and eight others, each of them building cottages within the year.[34]

Cabin on Lake Superior in the 1920s

THE ARROWHEAD

Except for those few persons able to purchase entire peninsulas or make arduous
treks over unimproved roads, Minnesota
lake residents of the 1910s and 1920s lived
in settings whose social and environmental
character underwent radical changes over
which they had little control. The advent of
the automobile, a thriving economy, and a
strong push from the state-funded Ten
Thousand Lake Association increased the
number of Minnesota tourists from thirteen
thousand in 1913 to forty thousand in 1918 to
more than three hundred thousand by 1921,
and the majority of these swarmed to resorts
and cabins on the state's lakes.[35]

For families that sought nature in small,
controlled doses and longed for a semblance
of civilization on remote sites, the transformation was welcome enough. But for the
rest, the lovers of wilderness unspoiled and
uncontrolled, most of the Lake Park Region
within reach of the great intercontinental
railroads was taking on too much urban
baggage. Their last refuge was the northeast

corner of the state, an area of dense lakes
and forests for the most part unpenetrated
by loggers or their transportation conduits.

The Arrowhead, as it came to be called,
was defined on the north by the boundary
waters between Minnesota and Canada, on
the southeast by Lake Superior, and on the
west by the Duluth, Virginia, and Rainy Lake
Railway connecting the tip of Lake Superior
to International Falls. Though remoteness
from early rail lines helped to postpone the
Arrowhead's exploitation, such railroads as
it had also first opened the touring public's
eyes to its wilderness values.

Completion of rail lines from Bemidji and
Duluth to International Falls in 1907 and
1909, respectively, immediately brought a
flurry of tourists to Rainy Lake and other
bodies of water along the international border. International Falls (formerly Koochi-
ching) crowed that "pleasure seekers come
here from all quarters to enjoy life to its
fullest extent."

One of the chief promoters of International Falls was the builder of its rail line from
Bemidji, lumber baron and land developer

Edward W. Backus. He and his partner per-
sonally escorted prominent Twin City and
Chicago visitors to the lake. Another leading
figure was H. I. Bedell, a homesteader on
Rainy Lake who developed four areas of
lakefront for summer cabins. In 1909, only
two years after Backus's Minnesota and
International Railway had reached town, a
guide promoting the International Falls area
boasted that four hundred "men of wealth"
purchased islands for summer homes as a
result of local promotion. Backus himself
built a summer house on a Rainy Lake island
in 1910, and his family and those of similar
social and financial stature came to be
known as the "Rainy Lake Aristocracy."[36]

One of the Rainy Lake summer residents
who did not fit the mold was Davenport,
Iowa, native Ernest Oberholtzer, whose cabin
was among the most daring log structures of
the period. Built on a steep hillside, its entry
façade was a single story composed largely
of porches, but the rear dropped an additional two stories, forming a tall, blocky mass
of logs with a cantilevered balcony. Trees
crowded against all sides of the cabin,

Thomas Filben cabin on Mukoota Lake at the start of demolition in 1989   *Jacob and Mina Casareto cabin on Crane Lake in 1989*

increasing the difficulty of initial construction and obstructing views to and from the finished structure. This was consistent with Oberholtzer's convictions as an outspoken conservationist. In the late 1920s, he parted ways with Backus and other local developers over proposals to dam some of the lakes in the Rainy Lake chain to form reservoirs. His long and ultimately successful fight paved the way for the strict conservation measures that have preserved much of the natural character of the land now comprising Voyageurs National Park and the Boundary Waters Canoe Area.

Wealthy summer residents also settled south and east of Rainy Lake. Among the most colorful of these was St. Paul's Thomas Filben. In the early 1920s, he and three of his brothers formed the Patrick Novelty Company and the J. M. Filben Company. Their main product was slot machines, but their business involved fencing for gangsters as much as it did retail trade. Filben's two-story log cabin on Trout Lake was so remote that it required a thirty-five-mile ride on a motorboat rented from a fishing lodge, followed by a portage and a final leg on another boat. None of this kept Filben from extravagantly furnishing his hideout—even to equipping it with a player piano.[37]

While tourism in the state as a whole crested in 1929, cabin and resort construction in the Rainy Lake chain continued unabated. Mina and Jacob Casareto came from Worth-ington, Minnesota, to summer on Crane Lake in a strange hodgepodge of a cabin begun around 1934 by three local woodworkers. Its profusion of dormers and patchwork of picture windows stemmed in equal measure from a strange beginning and a succession of additions and modifications. Craftsmanship of a far more sophisticated sort infused the design of Dr. Adolph Levin's cabin on Kabetogama Lake. Built with the assistance of two Finnish carpenters, its massive trusses and chimneys had a strong folk sensibility.[38]

A decade before the Rainy Lake region could boast of tourism, the Duluth and Iron Range rail line to Tower opened the center of the Arrowhead region to summer travel and settlement. By the mid-1890s, Lake Vermilion and the Ely area lakes were already enjoying their first large influx of tourists. Vermilion appeared poised to compete with the great tourist meccas of the Lake Park Region. It boasted a shoreline more than three times greater than Minnetonka's—longer, in fact, than the coastline of Lake Superior. Its 365 islands were unequaled in number by any other lake in Minnesota.

An outing club mixing Tower and Duluth residents with St. Paul sales representatives formed on Lake Vermilion in 1890 and began to construct cabins in the early 1900s. On a lake one-fourth its size on the Northern Pacific line, that would have spelled the beginning of summer settlements that sped around its shores. But the remoteness of the lake and the extraordinary difficulty of providing road access to any but its southernmost bays kept it from enjoying—or suffering—the post-World War I explosion of tourism that overtook the more centrally located northern lakes. In 1923 it could claim eight resorts, but that was a paltry figure for so large and convoluted a body of water.[39]

In spite of its failure to develop along the lines of lakes with far less natural potential, Lake Vermilion has its share of historic summer estates. Among the largest of these—if not the largest—was begun by leading Vir-

ginia citizen and iron mine developer Albert B. Coates. In 1911 Coates built an elaborate Craftsman summer house on Pike Bay, then followed it with an equally distinctive log bungalow for the use of his caretaker. Thirty

Dr. Adolph Levin cabin on Kabetogama Lake in 1989

Caretaker's cabin at the Albert B. Coates summer estate on Lake Vermilion in 1996

years later, his son, Albert Coates, Jr., hired a landscape architect and added a chauffeur's quarters and four-stall garage, butler's house, combined office and greenhouse, and boathouse. The latter, designed by Virginia architects Dambeck and Dambeck, had a recreation room and ballroom on the inshore side, a roof balcony overlooking the dock, and four boat slips designed for a rowboat, a motorboat, a yacht, and a power launch—all wrapped in a colonial revival shell. Each of the slips could be closed to the lake by an overhead door, the opening for the yacht running the full height of the mast.[40]

Close by the Coates property arose a log cabin equal in magnificence, if not size, to the great log lodges of the Brainerd area lakes. Said to be built for a Virginia dentist, its door hardware was hand-forged and wrought, exposed log beams tied the walls together at ceiling height, and a massive boulder fireplace stood against the end wall of the living room. These were all standard fare for architect-designed log cabins in the 1920s and 1930s. It was the pictorial touches that set the dentist's retreat apart. The logs

Albert Coates boathouse in 1996

A 1930s cabin on Pike Bay, Lake Vermilion, in 1997

Staircase of the Pike Bay cabin in 1997

ends were beveled and staggered in length, the windows were decoratively shuttered, and, most striking of all, the spindles of the interior staircase were each made from trunks of young birch trees, cut off just where the roots began to spread outward from the stem.

Minneapolis architect John Jager wrote colorful letters detailing the "sweat-sprinkled and depression-blistered issue" of his cabin-building labors on Wolf Island in Lake Vermilion. Addressed to his long-time friend, Prairie School architect William Purcell, the letters expressed joy and fatigue in equal measure. Shortly after beginning construction in 1929, Jager declared, "In view of workmanship it will be a real place. I hope it will not bankrupt me. It costs like blazes in hard cash and work."

Some of Jager's cabin-building pride and agony were the usual accompaniment of log and boulder construction at remote, northern Minnesota sites. But Jager pushed the process to its limits by making extraordinarily specific material choices. He began with a "cyclopean" foundation wall, hauling the largest boulders he could manage up the hill from the lakeshore with the aid of nothing more than a wheelbarrow. Cedar, red pine, and balsam fir logs each performed quite separate structural tasks reflecting their respective durability, strength, and appearance. Most of the logs were from the island itself, but some of the raw materials came out of Oregon forests or a Minneapolis lum-ber yard. The John F. Wilcox Company of Minneapolis supplied the millwork, and stone for the fireplace came from a recently opened local granite quarry. Four years after initial construction, Jager marveled that the logs still had not completely dried out, and he continued to work on the cabin and its landscaping for another decade.[41]

If any area of Minnesota answers to nineteenth-century notions of the sublime, it is the North Shore of Lake Superior. Craggy, steeply banked, alternately open and densely wooded, bounded by a lake that, from a visual perspective, could as well be an ocean, it has had a mystique all its own since the first lodge at Lutsen opened to guests in 1886. As in the towns at the ends of the lumbering routes, summering along the North Shore has followed its own course, with little physical connection to seasonal settlements and communities anywhere else. Lutsen's resort was more than eighty miles up the coast from Duluth and for forty years was accessible by boat alone.

As the Babcock Scenic Highway gradually opened in the 1920s, lodges, outing associa-tions, and private summer residences began to spring up along the shore. Forever safe from any commercial venture but fishing and tourism itself, the shoreline soon attracted sportsmen and wilderness trekkers from around the country. One of its largest summer colonies put down stakes on the Encampment River seven miles past Two Harbors, thirty-three northeast of Duluth. Known as the

"Cyclopean wall" of the John Jager cabin on Lake Vermilion in 1938

Encampment Forest Association Clubhouse in 1984

Encampment Forest Association, it was composed primarily of Minneapolis businessmen.

Encampment association members did not have far to go when it came time to design their cabins, for leading Minneapolis architect Edwin H. Hewitt was on the board of governors. How many availed themselves of his services has not been recorded, but the main lodge was constructed to Hewitt's plans in 1922-23. Cabin building proceeded in fits and starts for twenty years, until nineteen summer homes spread along the shore and riverbank. The earliest cabins were built from logs cut out of the 1,575-acre tract itself, but as the community grew, it became evident that continuing that practice would sacrifice an important element of its surroundings. Cabins after 1930 were, accordingly, built of log siding. What the cabins lost in nostalgic appeal they gained in durability, as encampment members gradually forsook rustic charm for up-to-date building practices.[42]

For many years the North Shore continued to exert an almost primeval force on architects and builders who worked its slopes. Through the 1940s and 1950s,

Edwin Lundie designed quiet masterpieces of timber-framed construction, each in the tentlike form that marked the first generation of lakeshore cottages in Minnesota. His work was marked with eccentricities—oversized stone chimneys, monumental turned columns, and an obsessive attention to interior detail—yet it also epitomized the quest for new approaches to traditional construction that have typified Lake Park Region summer cottages since the 1920s.

In recent decades the Arrowhead has become Minnesota's most active area in seasonal cabin construction. Year-round occupancy has become the rule at increasing numbers of lakes closer to urban centers or major highways. But the northeastern corner of the state retains enough forested wilderness to invite new generations of Minnesotans to establish their own places on a lake. Contemporary architects have responded to the challenge with a broad spectrum of traditionalist and modernist solutions. The objective remains the same as it was for the first builders on Lake Minnetonka, to retain and nurture a piece of civilization in the midst of solitude.

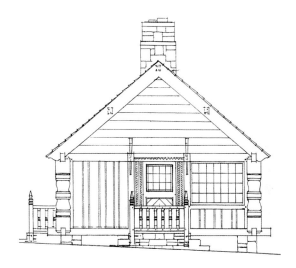

Edwin Lundie's elevation drawing of the Kromschroeder cabin on Lake Superior, 1945

149

# NOTES

SARATOGA OF THE WEST

[1] Henry Schoolcraft, "A Memoir of the History and Physical Geography of Minnesota," *Collections of the Minnesota Historical Society*, vol. 1 (St. Paul: Minnesota Historical Society, 1902), 90. Schoolcraft's essay was written for the historical society's first collection of papers, assembled between 1850 and 1856.

The Geology of Minnesota by N. H. Winchell, v. 1 (Minneapolis: State of Minnesota, 1884), 130, gave Schoolcraft's estimate the support of an unimpeachable authority. More accurate accounting has since pushed the number as high as 15,000, the precise figure depending on the criteria used to establish whether a given body of water is to be regarded as a lake.

[2] George Catlin, *Letters and Notes on the Manners, Customs, and Condition of the North American Indians*, vol. 2 (Philadelphia: 1857), and New York Tribune, June 20, 1854; both quoted by Theodore C. Blegen in "The 'Fashionable Tour' on the Upper Mississippi," *Minnesota History* 20 (Dec. 1939), 378-79, 386.

[3] *Minnesota Pioneer*, July 22, 1852, quoted by Blegen in "Fashionable Tour."

[4] Bettina A. Norton, *Edwin Whitefield: Nineteenth-Century North American Scenery* (Barre, Mass.: Barre Publishing Co., 1977), 15-16; Bertha L. Heilbron, "Edwin Whitefield, Settlers' Artist," *Minnesota History* 44 (Summer 1966), 62-69.

[5] Heilbron, "Edwin Whitefield," 74.

[6] John B. Bachelder, *Popular Resorts, and How to Reach Them. Combining a Brief Description of the Principal Summer Retreats in the United States, and the Routes of Travel Leading to Them* (Boston: John B. Bachelder, 1874). A more complete description of the Saratoga area was provided by E. R. Wallace's *Descriptive Guide to the Adirondacks, Land of the Thousand Lakes* (Syracuse, N.Y.: Bible Publishing House, 1887).

[7] John W. Bond, *Minnesota and Its Resources* (New York: Redfield, 1853), 237.

[8] Edward A. Bromley, *Minneapolis Album. A Photographic History of the Early Days in Minneapolis* (Minneapolis: Frank L. Thresher, 1890), unpaginated; Frank G. O'Brien, *Minnesota Pioneer Sketches* (Minneapolis: H.H.S. Rowell, 1904), 210-12; E. Dudley Parsons, *The Story of Minneapolis* (Minneapolis: Privately printed, 1913), 35-37. The famed Chalybeate Spring was located just below the site on which the Pillsbury A Mill was built.

[9] *Summer Resorts and Watering Places of the North-west, Illustrated; On Lines of the Chicago, Milwaukee, and St. Paul Railway* ([Milwaukee: Chicago, Milwaukee, and St. Paul Railway], 1874), 33; Franklyn Curtiss-Wedge, *History of Dakota and Goodhue Counties*, vol. 2 (Chicago: H. C. Cooper, Jr., and Co., 1910), 176-78.

[10] As a widely read law school graduate and "a peer among the finished gentlemen of the age," Garrard also entertained prominent easterners making a grand tour of the upper Mississippi, among them the architects Heins and La Farge and painter John LaFarge; Curtiss-Wedge, *History of Dakota and Goodhue Counties*, 176; Roger Kennedy, *Minnesota Houses, An Architectural and Historical View* (Minneapolis: Dillon Press, 1967), 16-17.

[11] "The Abuses of Summer," *Frank Leslie's Illustrated Newspaper*, Sept 8, 1888. Even with modern expectations of city-style conveniences, proximity to a body of water and a similitude of rural life remain the chief criteria for choice of a summer home site in Minnesota as they are through much of the upper Midwest; see Richard L. Ragnatz, "The Vacation Home Market: An Analysis of the Spatial Distribution of Population on a Seasonal Basis," Ph.D. diss., Cornell University, 1969.

[12] See "In an Adirondack Idyll: The Brahmins of Follesby" by R. Lynn Matson, *Nineteenth Century*, Spring 1977, p. 18-25.

[13] See, for example, *Guide and Directory of Lake Minnetonka, Minnesota* (Excelsior, Minn.: H.W. Mowry, 1884; reprint Excelsior: E. Wright, 1983) and Daniel S.

Reiff, "Smaller Camps of the Adirondacks," *Nineteenth Century* 12 ([Spring] 1993): 23-29. Reiff employed a taxonomy of Adirondack dwelling types quite different from what I have developed here.

[14] "Hickory Rustic Work," *Lake Minnetonka Tourist*, June 1876.

MINNETONKA: A LAKE FOR POETS AND PLEASURE SEEKERS

[1] In a curious lapse of memory, the editor of the *Saint Anthony Express* published an account of Eli Pettijohn's "discovery" of the forty-mile-long (*sic*) lake on Mar. 20, then credited Tuttle, who relied on Pettijohn's tips for his exploration, with it on Apr. 16. See also Nicholas E. Duff, *Maplewoods* (Privately printed, 1996), 4-5. Copies of Duff's booklet are in Wayzata Public Library and the Minnesota Historical Society research center (MHS).

[2] *Weekly Minnesotian*, Sept. 11, 1852; *Northwestern Tourist*, Aug. 25, 1887.

[3] "Lake Minnetonka," *Tourist and Sportsman*, May 24, 1879; Duff, *Maplewoods*, 5; *Weekly Minnesotian*, Sept. 11 and 18, 1852; S. E. Ellis, *Souvenir and Story of the Most Popular Summer Resort in the Northwest, Lake Minnetonka* (Minneapolis: S. E. Ellis, 1905).

[4] Mrs. Clarkson Lindley, "Maplewood," in *Historical Reminiscences of Lake Minnetonka* (N.p.: Lake Minnetonka Garden Club, [1946?]), 29-31; *Tourist*, June 19, 1880. An ad in *Tourist and Sportsman*, Aug. 24, 1878, indicates that Gale had attempted to get out of the hostelry business some years earlier.

[5] Duff, *Maplewoods*, 14; Thelma Jones, *Once Upon a Lake* (Minneapolis: Ross and Haines, 1969), 304. According to Lindley, the land was originally pre-empted by the Guilds and parts sold off to Gale, which was a highly unlikely scenario given Samuel Gale's

early and persistent pursuit of Lake Minnetonka land and the connection of the Guilds to Minnetonka through Gale's wife. Even the Guilds may have been preceded by many years as summer residents on the lake by a New Jersey native, W. A. Jackson. A friend of the legendary Halsteads, Jackson was reported in 1877 to be "one of the old time residents, when Lake Minnetonka was unknown to the world." He proved his familiarity with the lake by acting as guide and historian to a party of visitors to the Hermitage. How and where the Jacksons stayed at the lake is not reported; see *Tourist and Sportsman*, July 28, 1877.

[6] The first modern writer to claim Samuel and Susan Gale's priority was their daughter, Mrs. Clarkson Lindley, in "Maplewood," 30. Her claim has been reiterated many times, e.g., by Ellen Wilson Meyer in *Tales from Tonka* (Excelsior, Minn.: Excelsior-Lake Minnetonka Historical Society, 1993), 52.

[7] Wildwood's popularity was noted many times by local newspaperman A. S. Dimond during the summer that Maplewood was fitted out as a resort; see, for example, *Lake Minnetonka Tourist*, July 15, 1876.

[8] Isabel Thibault, "My Island: Memories of a Childhood on Gale's Island," typescript paper sponsored by the Excelsior-Lake Minnetonka Historical Society, 1978. A copy is at MHS. See also *Lake Minnetonka Tourist*, June 6 and July 29, 1876; *Tourist and Sportsman*, Mar. 10, 1877.

[9] All of these anecdotes are based on the memories of Harlow Gale's son, also named Harlow; Jones, *Once Upon a Lake*, 366.

[10] L. U. Reavis, *St. Louis: The Future Great City of the World* (St. Louis: L. R. Barns, 1876), 493; *Lake Minnetonka Tourist*, Aug. 19 and 26, 1876; *Tourist and Sportsman*, June 16, 1877.

[11] Helen Hunt Bennett, "Northome," in *Historical Reminiscences of Lake Minnetonka*, 25.

[12] Reavis, *St. Louis*, 494; Bennett, "Northome," 25-26. Oral tradition provides that a Boston firm did the landscaping, and that is usually taken to mean Olmsted. The project does not appear in any published list of his work.

[13] *Tourist and Sportsman*, July 20, 1878, and May 24, 1879.

[14] *Tourist and Sportsman*, May 24 and May 31, 1879; Duff, *Maplewoods*, 15. The Hatch cottage is often identified as the second summer residence on the lake, apparently under the assumption that Woolsey's octagon house was built for Samuel Gale; see, for example,

Jones, *Once Upon a Lake*, 240. But the Gale family's stays at Maplewood through the late 1870s, well documented in the local papers, argue otherwise.

[15] *Tourist and Sportsman*, June 30, 1877; *Lake Minnetonka Tourist*, Sept. 20, 1876; *Tourist and Sportsman*, Aug. 18, 1877.

[16] *Northwestern Tourist*, Sept. 21, 1889.

[17] *A Guide for Tourists, Sportsmen, and Invalids* (Minneapolis: Wilcox and Dimond, 1879), 15; [Minneapolis] *Real Estate Review*, Aug. 1887 and Feb. 1888; *Northwestern Tourist*, May 17, 1884, and July 1, 1885; *Tourist and Sportsman*, Aug. 1895.

[18] *Real Estate Review*, Feb. 1888; *Northwestern Tourist*, May 20, 1886, and July 16, 1892; *Illustrated Minneapolis, Souvenir of the Minneapolis Journal* (Minneapolis: Minneapolis Journal, 1891), 46.

[19] Ellen Wilson Meyer, *Picturesque Deephaven* (Excelsior, Minn.: Excelsior-Minnetonka Historical Society, 1989), 101; *Northwestern Tourist*, Aug. 2, 1890.

[20] *Summer Resorts of Minnesota*, 12. The local paper changed names many times; in 1877 to the *Tourist and Sportsman*, in 1880 to the *Tourist*, in 1881 back to the *Tourist and Sportsman*, in 1883 to the *Northwestern Tourist*, and in 1895, its final year, back once again to *Tourist and Sportsman*. The place of publication oscillated between Minneapolis and Excelsior, though events in the Excelsior area always drew its primary attention.

[21] *Lake Minnetonka Tourist*, July 8 and Aug. 26, 1876; *Tourist and Sportsman*, May 31, 1879. Mrs. Clark's addition of 1879 was reported to be a "Swiss" cottage.

[22] Francisca Schaefer Winston, "Excelsior," in *Historical Reminiscences of Lake Minnetonka*, 21. Winston claims that the Lymans and Hales were the first Minneapolis families to build cottages in Excelsior.

[23] *Tourist and Sportsman*, Aug. 3, 1878, and June 5, 1880; *American Traveler's Journal* 2 (Aug. 1881): 6.

[24] *Tourist and Sportsman*, May 24, 1879.

[25] *Tourist and Sportsman*, May 24, 1879; Jones, *Once Upon a Lake*, 246; *American Traveler's Journal* 2 (Aug. 1881): 5.

[26] *Tourist and Sportsman*, May 24, 1879, and Feb. 19 and Apr. 30, 1882.

[27] *American Traveler's Journal* 2 (Aug. 1881): 5.

[28] *Lake Minnetonka Tourist*, Aug. 26, 1876.

[29] *Tourist and Sportsman*, Aug. 4, 1877, and May 4, 1878; Jones, *Once Upon a Lake*, 319-20, 250-51.

[30] Jones, *Once Upon a Lake*, 251-52, 320.

[31] *St. Paul and Minneapolis Pioneer Press*, Dec. 11, 1885; *Northwest Architect and Improvement Record*, June

1887; Jones, *Once Upon a Lake*, 320; *Excelsior Cottager*, Apr. 16, 1897.

[32] *Tourist and Sportsman*, June 6, 1882. Meyer, "Mr. Bracket and His Bean-Hole Beans," in *Tales from Tonka*, 87-90. Brackett's enormous contribution to the people and city of Minneapolis are amply documented by Isaac Atwater in *History of the City of Minneapolis* (New York: Munsell and Co., 1893), 240-45.

[33] Meyer claimed that Brackett's peninsula anchored one point of the triangular race, but this is not borne out by printed maps of the races, at least after the yacht clubhouse was built in 1892.

[34] *Tourist and Sportsman*, May 24, 1879; Bergmann Richards, *The Early Background of Minnetonka Beach* (Minneapolis: Hennepin County Historical Society, 1957), 66; George W. Cooley, *Map of Lake Minnetonka*, 1892. Several charming stories of Northwood life are related in a typescript paper by Margaret E. Jackson, on file at the Long Lake-Western Hennepin County Museum. Some have been retold by Jones, *Once Upon a Lake*, 345-50.

[35] *Northwestern Tourist*, Sept. 3, 1882. A German visitor, Nicolaus Mohr, put the Lafayette's charms in perspective when he published an account of his American excursions. While averring that it was indeed "a gigantic wood building, lofty, simple, clean, but not luxurious, with huge covered terraces and spacious salons," what it really reminded him of was the sort of structure his countrymen would erect for a sports tournament or song fest; Nicolaus Mohr, *Excursion Through America*, trans. by La Vern J. Ripley (Chicago: R.R. Donnelley and Sons Co., 1973), 79.

[36] Richards, *Minnetonka Beach*, 86-90; *Northwestern Tourist*, Aug. 23, 1884.

[37] A much-chastened Henry house achieved national coverage when Prairie School architects Purcell and Elmslie did a mild but effective remodeling of it for second owner Charles W. Sexton; *Western Architect* 19 (Jan. 1913).

[38] Grace Bliss Dayton, "Upper Lake Minnetonka," in *Historical Reminiscences of Lake Minnetonka*, 13-14; D. H. Ogden, *The Summer Resorts of Minnesota* (Cedar Rapids, Ia.: D. H. Ogden, 1878), 12.

[39] Grace Dayton, 12-13. See also Ellen Wilson Meyer, "The Halsteads: Hermits of Minnetonka," in *Historical Reminiscences of Lake Minnetonka*, 59-62. Both accounts summarize lore first surfacing in numerous tales of the two Halsteads published in local newspapers at the time of their deaths.

[40] *Lake Minnetonka Tourist*, Aug. 12, 1876; *Tourist and Sportsman*, Apr. 7, 1877.

[41] "Builded at Minnetonka"; Theodore Blegen, *The Saga of Saga Hill* (La Crosse, Wis.: Sumac Press, 1970), 294-95.

[42] *Lake Minnetonka Tourist*, Aug. 26, 1876; *Tourist and Sportsman*, May 24, 1879.

[43] *Tourist and Sportsman*, July 28, 1877.

[44] Zimmerman's first visit to the lake had been a professional one, to photograph its scenery for stereopticon views; *Tourist and Sportsman*, Apr. 3, 1877, and May 24, 1879; *Tourist*, June 5, 1880.

[45] *Northwestern Tourist*, Sept. 7 and Sept 21, 1889, and Aug. 9, 1890.

[46] *Tourist and Sportsman*, June 11, 1881; United States Census, Minnesota, 1880 and 1890, microfilm at MHS; *Guide and Directory of Lake Minnetonka, Minnesota*, 24.

[47] Deed records, Office of the Recorder, Hennepin County Courthouse, Minneapolis; *St. Paul Globe*, Dec. 24, 1882; numerous issues of *Tourist and Sportsman*, 1880-82.

[48] *Tourist and Sportsman*, June 5, 1880, and Aug. 9, 1882.

[49] *Tourist and Sportsman*, Aug. 9, 1882; Dayton, "Upper Lake Minnetonka," 14-15; Jones, *Once Upon a Lake*, 268.

[50] Jones, *Once Upon a Lake*, 368-69; Meyer, *Tales from Tonka*, 103.

[51] O. N. Nelson, *History of the Scandinavians and Successful Scandinavians in the United States*, vol. 2 (Minneapolis: O. N. Nelson Co., 1904), 485-86; Jones, *Once Upon a Lake*, 367.

[52] *Home-Builder* 1 (Jan. 1899), 29-30. This was the first volume of what became *Keith's Magazine*, a patternbook-oriented periodical produced by Minneapolis architect-builder Walter J. Keith.

[53] F. H. Nutter, "'Highcroft,' Lake Minnetonka Minn.," *Western Architect* 3 (Feb. 1903): 10-11; Jones, *Once Upon a Lake*, 325.

[54] Jones, *Once Upon a Lake*, 326, 333.

[55] Jones's office renderings of half a dozen of these early Minnetonka designs were published as a display spread in *American Architect*, Jan. 30, 1892.

[56] Edith D. Williams, "The House of the Month: An Interesting View of a Minnetonka Estate Very Nearly Selected as the Summer White House," *Amateur Golfer and Sportsman* 5 (Dec. 1929): 24-26.

[57] *Brickbuilder* 21 (May 1912); Jones, *Once Upon a Lake*, 310-11; Meyer, *Tales from Tonka*, 175.

[58] Deborah S. Haight, "The Littles and Their Architect," in *Frank Lloyd Wright: The Library from the Francis W. Little House* (Allentown, Penn.: Allentown Art Museum, 1978), 13-14.

WHITE BEAR:
A PEARL SET IN EMERALD

[1] *Minnesota Pioneer*, quoted by J. Fletcher Williams in *A History of the City of Saint Paul and of the County of Ramsey, Minnesota*, vol. 4 of the *Collections of Minnesota Historical Society* (St. Paul: Minnesota Historical Society, 1876), 301, and Nancy Woolworth in *The White Bear Lake Story* (White Bear Lake: White Bear Lake Area Chamber of Commerce, 1968), 14, 16-17.

[2] Woolworth, *White Bear*, 15, 17. Woolworth claimed that St. Paul young people spent "summer vacations" at the lake, but newspaper stories record only day trips or overnights. She also overstated the patronage from eastern and southern states; with only two small hotels open in the 1850s, the capacity of the lake community for hosting long-term stays was still severely limited.

[3] "Minnesota's Gem: White Bear Lake," *Tourist and Sportsman*, Apr. 7, 1877; map of White Bear Lake in *Northwestern Tourist*, Sept. 1, 1883.

[4] H. P. Robinson, "At White Bear Lake: A Glance at St. Paul's Charming Summer Resort," *Northwest Magazine*, July 1885, p. 19.

[5] D. H. Ogden, *Summer Resorts*, 13.

[6] "Minnesota's Gem"; *Tourist and Sportsman*, Sept. 9, 1879.

[7] *Tourist and Sportsman*, July 28 and Sept. 15, 1877, May 4, 1878, and May 24 and 31, 1879.

[8] Display advertisement in *St. Paul and Minneapolis Pioneer Press*, Dec. 12, 1882; *Tourist and Sportsman*, May 24, 1879; Robinson, "At White Bear," 22. The Walter Mann summer cottage was probably also built to Buffington's plans, as he had recently designed Mann's new house in St. Paul.

[9] T. M. Newson, *Indian Legends of White Bear, Lake Pepin, and Lake Elmo* (Minneapolis: Dimond and Ross, 1881), 8; William W. Cutler, "Charles Phelps Noyes," *Minnesota History Bulletin* 4 (Aug.-Nov. 1921): 114. In recent times, the Noyes cottage is usually referred to as the Fillebrown house, after the family that donated it to the White Bear Lake Historical Society.

[10] *American Travelers Journal* ? (Aug. 1881): 11, 13; Newson, *Indian Legends*, 9.

[11] *St. Paul and Minneapolis Pioneer Press*, Apr. 30, 1882; *Tourist and Sportsman*, Mar. 20 and Apr. 16, 1882. The choice of Millard over Bassford was a victory of art over economy.

[12] *Tourist and Sportsman*, Mar. 20 and May 7, 1882.

[13] The summer community never expanded much beyond the eight houses and three communal buildings shown on the map "Environs of St. Paul, Village of White Bear" in *Atlas of the Environs of St. Paul and Ramsey County* (Philadelphia: G. M. Hopkins, 1886). According to a common oral tradition, Gilbert's design was done for St. Paul dentist R. W. Berthel, who may have been the second owner of the cottage. Galusha's name appears on the 1886 map and again at the head of a letter written by plumbing contractor W. J. Dyer to Gilbert in 1884. I am indebted to Jan Forsberg for showing me this letter, which is in the Cass Gilbert Papers, MHS.

[14] Woolworth, *White Bear*, 12.

[15] Carl B. Drake, *Recollections of Manitou Island, White Bear Lake, Minnesota* (N. p.: McGill-Warner Co., 1957), 6; *St. Paul and Minneapolis Pioneer Press*, Apr. 30, 1882.

[16] *Tourist and Sportsman*, Apr. 9, 1882; Drake, *Recollections*, 8.

[17] Larson, *Minnesota Architect*, 39; Robinson, "At White Bear Lake," 22.

[18] *St. Paul Globe*, Dec. 31, 1882; *St. Paul and Minneapolis Pioneer Press*, Nov. 18, 1882; *Northwestern Tourist*, July 7, 1883; *Tourist and Sportsman*, July 28, 1877. The original E. C. Palmer house was brought up to the size of its companions by several late-nineteenth-century additions; see Drake, *Recollections*, 15.

[19] "White Bear Improvements," *St. Paul and Minneapolis Pioneer Press*, Jan. 10 (?), 1886; *Northwest Tourist*, July 7, 1883.

[20] The Minnetonka cottages were Northome, the John Noble cottage at Covington, the A. A. Pond villa at Fairview, the Walpole cottage and Moore villa at Cottagewood, the C. H. Prior and F. C. Pillsbury villas in Ferndale, the G. A. Brackett cottage at Orono Point, and the Huntington-Potter cottage in Northwood. No summer community at Minnetonka held more than two cottages in this price bracket. The 1882 notice of Johnston's White Bear Lake commissions gave the average cost as "above 3,500." Changes that drove up the average almost 50 percent higher may account for the late completion dates.

[21] Drake, *Recollections*, 8, 15.

22 Drake, *Recollections*, 20.

23 See Patricia A. Murphy, "The Early Career of Cass Gilbert: 1878 to 1895" (Master's thesis, University of Virginia, 1979). Photographs of the Morton and Tarbox cottages taken shortly after completion were published in the supplement to the *Northwest Builder and Decorator*, 1890, plates 180 and 181, respectively. Gilbert's rendering of the Morton house appeared earlier in *American Architect and Building News*, May 23, 1891. Notice of Gilbert planning a $2,500 cottage for Tracy Lyon was published in *Improvement Bulletin*, Feb. 22, 1896, but cottagers, just like their city equivalents, often changed architects. The Peet cottage footprint appeared on the 1886 map but not on atlases from 1898 and thereafter.

24 "Dellwood, White Bear Lake, Minnesota" (privately printed by Hiler H. Horton and A. K. Barnum, 1888), in MHS; Robinson, "At White Bear," 21.

25 *Northwestern Tourist*, July 7, 1883; Robinson, "At White Bear," 21. The Barnum house was Gilbert's first design at White Bear Lake and one of the first projects of the St. Paul phase of his career. A drawing was published in *American Architect* in 1885.

26 Newspaper clipping in the Truman W. Ingersoll Papers at MHS, cited by Patricia Condon Johnston in "Truman Ingersoll: St. Paul Photographer Pictured the World," *Minnesota History* 47 (Winter 1980): 129. The identity of the Ordway cabin is established by notes in Ingersoll's photograph albums of Birch Lodge, also at MHS.

27 Johnston, "Ingersoll," 129.

28 L. S. Buffington also frequented the most fashionable spots at both lakes; perhaps the practice was commonplace among architects who depended on highly placed social contacts for their commissions.

29 Edith Cums, "The Home of the Month: An Intimate View of the Beautiful Estate of Mr. and Mrs. E. N. Saunders, Jr., at Dellwood," *Amateur Golfer and Sportsman* 5 (Nov. 1929): 36.

30 Robinson, "At White Bear," 22.

31 A. M. Cleland, *Minnesota Lakes* (St. Paul: Northern Pacific Railway, 1906), 15; Woolworth, *White Bear*, 40; *St. Paul and Minneapolis Pioneer Press*, Jan. 10, 1886.

WATERING HOLES
IN THE GARDEN OF THE WEST

1 *Tourists' Guide of the Northwest* (Milwaukee: Chicago, Milwaukee and St. Paul Railroad, 1879), 82-83; *Tourist and Sportsman*, June 8, 1878; *Independent Farmer and Fireside Companion* 1 (1879), 136.

2 For a list of "perfected" resort lakes promoted by the Milwaukee Road, see *Inland Architect and New Record* 19 (July 1992): xxii. A humorous but accurate account of the competition to boat from one watershed to the other is given by Evan Jones in *The Minnesota: Forgotten River* (New York: Holt, Rinehart and Winston, 1962), 110-11.

3 "Lake Elmo: A Foliage Embowered Gem," *St. Paul and Minneapolis Pioneer Press*, Apr. 30, 1882. On July 30, 1882, the same paper published a notice of plans being prepared for a "Lake Elmo summer residence for Dr. Walther to cost $2,000." Building notices for so rural a location were extremely rare.

4 "The Western Prairie Garden," *Tourist and Sportsman*, May 24, 1879.

5 *Tourist and Sportsman*, May 24, 1879; *Shakopee Tribune*, Apr. 30, 1897.

6 For the preeminence of the leading three resort communities, see "Our Rural Homes," *Tourist and Sportsman*, Mar. 10, 1877.

7 Franklyn Curtiss-Wedge, *History of Wright County, Minnesota* (Chicago: H. C. Cooper, Jr., and Co., 1915), v. 1: 227; *Annandale, Minnesota: A Community of Spirit* (Annandale: Annandale Centennial Committee, 1988), 38.

8 Lotus Heaton Williams, "Memories of Annandale," 1904, p. 11, copy of typescript in the collections of Wright County Historical Society.

9 Williams, "Memories," 12.

10 Murray obituary in *St. Paul Dispatch*, Dec. 8, 1906; Williams, "Memories," 11.

11 Curtiss-Wedge, *Wright County*, v. 1: 434-35.

12 Unless otherwise noted, all the information on Coney Island is drawn from *Waconia, Paradise of the Northwest: The Lake and Its Island* (Waconia, Minn.: Waconia Heritage Association, 1986), 85-108.

13 *Carver County News*, Aug. 8, 1890, quoted in *Waconia*, 85.

14 *Compendium of History and Biography of Carver and Hennepin Counties, Minnesota* (Chicago: Henry Taylor and Co., 1915), 240.

15 Cleland, *Minnesota Lakes*, 15.

16 A. S. Dimond, *The Magic Northland: An Illustrated Guide for Tourists to the New Northwest* (Minneapolis: Hoppin, Palmer and Dimond, 1881), 104. The attribution to Gilbert is in a note on the back of a photographic print donated by a Hummel descendant to MHS. The Hummel cottage would have been designed during a period when Gilbert's dwindling St. Paul practice was almost entirely in the hands of his chief assistant, Thomas Holyoke; so if his office did handle the commission, it most likely fell to Holyoke or one of the other draftsmen rather than Gilbert himself.

17 Dimond, *The Magic Northland*, 105.

18 These and other details about the Schwyzer estate on Grindstone Lake are all drawn from a letter from Hanns C. Schwyzer to Mark E. Haidet, Jan. 16, 1980, in the Arnold Schwyzer papers, MHS.

19 There were probably several others. First person stories of the kennel club's social life are related in "Early Days of North St. Paul," a taped interview made by the Ramsey County Historical Society on Oct. 12, 1954, and transcribed by S. B. Cleland in 1959; a building start notice for D. J. Egleston's cottage appeared in *St. Paul and Minneapolis Pioneer Press*, Nov. 18, 1882; Reeve's farm and residence were noted by A. S. Diamond in *The Magic Northland*, 80.

20 David Lanegran and Ernest R. Sandeen, *The Lake District of Minneapolis: A History of the Calhoun-Isles Community* (St. Paul: Living History Museum, 1979), 16-17.

21 Lanegran and Sandeen, *The Lake District*, 102-4.

22 For a brief account of the conversion of Lake Pulaski resorts to summer cabins, see Marcia Paulson, *Buffalo: From Trading Post to Star City* (Buffalo, Minn.: Buffalo Centennial Committee, 1987), 119-21.

LAKES WITHOUT NUMBER

1 Thomas Canfield, president of the Northern Pacific Railroad, at first restricted his description of the area to the lakes clustered in Becker and Otter Tail Counties; *Illustrated Album of Biography of the Famous Red River of the North and the Park Region* (Chicago: Alden, Ogle, and Co., 1889), 836.

2 "Minnesota as a Summer Resort," *Tourist and Sportsman*, June 8, 1878.

3 "Detroit Among the Lakes," *Northwest Magazine*, July 1885.

4 "Detroit Among the Lakes"; "Hotel Minnesota, the New Summer Resort of the Northwest," advertising brochure, 1884, MHS; *Album of Views in and about the Detroit Lakes, the Popular Summer Resort of Northern Minnesota* (Detroit, Minn.: Detroit Lakes and Pelican Valley Navigation Co., [1896]).

5 Ken Prentice, *Horse and Buggy Days at Detroit Lakes* (Detroit Lakes: Lakes Publishing Co., 1971), 73, 75; *Album of Views in and about the Detroit Lakes*.

6 Prentice, *Detroit Lakes*, 29, 31; Alvin H. Wilcox, *A Pioneer History of Becker County, Minnesota* (St. Paul: Pioneer Press Co., 1907), 334, 340, 724, 736; U.S. Census, 1900, Minnesota.

7 Bertha Heilbron, "Edwin Whitefield's Minnesota Lakes, " *Minnesota History*, Summer 1953, p. 251.

8 *Illustrated Album of Biography*, 836; Frank Jacobs, *Pelican Rapids Diamond Jubilee* (Pelican Rapids, Minn.: Privately printed, 1958).

9 *Tourist and Sportsman*, June 5, 1880; "From the Park Region," *Tourist and Sportsman*, June 11, 1881; *Northwestern Tourist*, Aug. 25, 1883.

10 *The Lady of the Lakes, Alexandria Minnesota* (Alexandria, Minn.: Alexandria Post News, 1900), 8.

11 Hannah Bartlett Ford, *A Part of Us: A Conversational History of the Minnesouri Angling Club* (N.p: Privately printed, 1986), 1-3, 28.

12 The information regarding Lake Whipple and Green Lake is drawn from numerous unindexed promotional brochures in the county files of MHS collections. They are also frequently referred to and briefly described in turn-of-the-century railroad brochures, e.g., Great Northern's *Beauty Spots* and Northern Pacific's *Minnesota Lakes*.

13 *History of Spicer on Green Lake* (N.p.: s.n., [1991]), 151; telephone interview with Allen Latham, June 14, 1997. According to Latham, the current owner of Medayto, the cottage was the family's primary residence from the beginning. But like the Guilds on Lake Minnetonka, they spent the coldest winter months in town.

14 Interview with Latham, who cited the Tolman cottage on Crescent Beach as the first pure summer residence on the lake, an indication of how completely the nineteenth-century settlement referred to in railroad brochures has been lost, apparently even to memory.

15 By the turn of the century, only Deerwood, fourteen miles east of Brainerd, had established a substantial summer colony. The town sat directly on the Northern Pacific line and within three miles of thirty lakes; *Minnesota Lakes*, 15.

16 *Minnesota Lakes*, 19

17 *Northwest Magazine*, July 1888, p. 16; "Brainerd, the City of the Pines," *Minneapolis Sunday Tribune*, Apr. 17, 1887.

18 Marjorie Wilson Richison, *Living Near to Nature's Heart: The History of the Pelican Lake Outing Club, 1902-1992* (Norman, Okla.: Kingswood Publishing Co., 1992), 21-23.

19 E. R. Mockett's diary, quoted in Richison, *Nature's Heart*, 55-57.

20 A photo album showing both Mrs. Osborn's cabin and the cottages associated with it is in MHS collections.

21 Tom Jardine, "All Bets Were Off When Luther Youngdahl Declared War on Minnesota Gamblers," *Twin Cities*, April 1983; Richison, *Nature's Heart*, 148.

22 For more details regarding the planning and construction of the Fawcett summer house, see Robert Frame's National Register of Historic Places (NRHP) nomination of the Wilford H. Fawcett house, 1980, and accompanying photographs, copy in the State Historic Preservation Office, MHS.

23 *Fortune* 5 (May 1932): 68-69; Robert Frame, NRHP nomination of Shawano House, 1980, copy in the State Historic Preservation Office.

24 Duane R. Lund, *Tales of Four Lakes: Leech Lake, Gull Lake, Mille Lacs Lake, the Red Lakes* (Staples, Minn.: Nordell Graphic Communications, 1986), 84; *It Happened Here* (Brainerd, Minn.: Brainerd Journal Press, 1948), 28-29.

25 "Physical Description of Floyd B. Olson Summer House," typescript notes by Charles Nelson in the State Historic Preservation Office. It is possible that the great hall addition matched its materials to the original structure, rather than the original adopting new facings to match the addition, but the crafted detail and composition of the facings reflects a period practice far commoner in the late 1920s and 1930s than in the World War I era.

26 Lund, *Tales of Four Lakes*, 46.

27 Carol Crawford Ryan, "Summering: Everyday Life in a Vacation Community, 1909-1985," Ph.D. diss., University of Minnesota, 1987, p. 64-65; *Cass Lake— "The Permanent Home of the Pine"* (Cass Lake, Minn.: Cass Lake Commercial Club, 1920).

28 Ryan, "Summering," 76-78; Carol Crawford Ryan, "Saving Star Island," *Minnesota History* 48 (Fall 1982): 109, 117.

29 Ryan, "Summering," 66; *St. Paul Daily News*, Mar. 20, 1927.

30 "Sheshebe Point, Lake Minnewawa," sales brochure printed for the Tingdale Brothers in 1913; MHS collections.

31 Most of the information for this paragraph comes from poring over the photographs in the collections of the Itasca County Historical Society in Grand Rapids. The pictures of summer residences are evenly divided between cabins used by small groups of men and those used by families.

32 The building description is drawn from pictures and notes in the Nadine Martin scrapbook in the collections of Itasca County Historical Society.

33 Bill Marshall, "The Joyce Estate," *Itasca County Historical Society Newsletter* 13 (Winter 1989).

34 "New Building Booms at Lake Resort," *St. Paul Daily News*, May 1, 1927.

35 Dona Sanford, "Growth of Minnesota Tourism and Recreation in the Northern Great Lakes Region of Minnesota, 1890-1945," 14. I am indebted to Mary Graves, historian for Voyageur National Park, for showing me a draft of this unpublished study. Much of the following material is taken from that study, checked and supplemented by Minneapolis directories and biographies.

36 Sanford, "Growth of Minnesota Tourism," 12-13, 16.

37 Paul Maccabee, *John Dillinger Slept Here* (St. Paul: MHS, 1995), 71-75; St. Paul City Directories.

38 Much of the information from this paragraph is taken from a survey in progress of extant summer cabins on Voyageur National Park land; Voyageur National Park headquarters, International Falls.

39 Stephen Hennessey, *The Life and Times of the Vermilion Club* (Scottsdale, Ariz.: Leadership, Inc., 1993); [C. M. Barr], *Nature's Playground* (Duluth: Privately printed, 1923).

40 Interview with John Swift, Lake Vermilion, August 10, 1996; working drawings of boathouse for Albert Coates. The descriptions are based on personal observation.

41 Letters and notes to William G. Purcell, Aug. 30, 1929, Sept. 4, 1933, and Oct. 23, 1938, Northwest Architectural Archives, St. Paul.

42 Joseph R. Kingman, *History of Encampment Forest Association* (N.p.: Privately printed, [1945]), 8-9, 23-24.

INDEX

ILLUSTRATION CREDITS

jacket front. Allen Latham
jacket back. MHS
half-title page. Ann Luther
frontispiece. Carver County
               Historical Society
9. *Western Architect*, Minneapolis
    Public Library
11. Minnesota Historical Society (MHS)
13. MHS
14. *Minneapolis Minnen*, private collection
15. *Popular Resorts and How to Reach Them*, MHS
16. MHS
17. Roger Kennedy photo, MHS
18. *Frank Leslie's Sunday Magazine*, University of Minnesota Libraries
19*l*. Jacoby photo, MHS
19*r*. MHS
20. MHS
21*t*. *Frank Leslie's Illustrated Newspaper*, University of Minnesota Libraries
21*b*. MHS
22. Itasca County Historical Society
23. *Northwest Magazine*, MHS
24*t*. *Northwestern Architect, Builder and Decorator*, MHS
24*b*. Private collection
25. *Western Architect*, Minneapolis Public Library
27. C. J. Hibbard photo, MHS
28. John S. Small map, *Hennepin County History*, MHS
30. *Tourist and Sportsman*, MHS
31. Wittemann Brothers engraving, *Lake Minnetonka*, MHS
32. *History of Minneapolis*, private collection
33. *Minneapolis – A Quarterly Magazine*, MHS
34. *St. Louis: The Future Great City of the World*, MHS
35. MHS
36. MHS
38. W. H. Jacoby photo, MHS
39*l*. Paul Larson photo
39*r*. *Illustrated Minneapolis*, Minneapolis Public Library
40. *Picturesque Lake Minnetonka*, Minneapolis Public Library
43. *Minneapolis Minnen*, private collection
44. MHS
45. *Northwestern Architect and Improvement Record*, Northwest Architectural Archives
46. Lachlen and Martha Reed and West Hennepin County Pioneers Association
47. L. D. Sweet photo, MHS
49. Paul Larson photo
50. *Northwestern Builder and Decorator*, MHS
51. *American Architect*, Minneapolis Public Library
52. L. D. Sweet photo, *Picturesque Lake Minnetonka*, MHS
53. *Picturesque Lake Minnetonka*, Minneapolis Public Library
54. MHS
55. Minnetonka-Excelsior Historical Society
56. Wittemann Brothers engraving, *Lake Minnetonka*, MHS
57. *Northwestern Builder and Decorator*, MHS
58. *Picturesque Lake Minnetonka*, Minneapolis Public Library
59. *Art Glimpses of Minneapolis, the City of Homes*, private collection
60. *Western Architect*, Minneapolis Public Library
62. *Northwestern Architect*, Northwest Architectural Archives
63. *Western Architect*, Minneapolis Public Library
64. Western Architect, Minneapolis Public Library
65*l*. *Illustrated Minneapolis*, Minneapolis Public Library
65*r*. Harry W. Jones collection, Hennepin County Historical Society
66. Private collection
67. *Architectural Record*, Minneapolis Public Library
68*l*. *Architectural Record*, Minneapolis Public Library
68*r*. Mr. and Mrs. Raymond Stevenson
69. Northwest Architectural Archives
71. Truman W. Ingersoll photo, MHS
72. *Northwestern Tourist*, MHS
75. Paul Larson photo
77. MHS
78. Paul Larson photo (retinted)
80. *Northwestern Architect, Builder, and Decorator*, MHS
82. Paul Larson photo
83. *Northwestern Builder and Decorator*, MHS
84. *Northwestern Builder and Decorator*, MHS
85. Buckbee-Mears photo, MHS
86. Truman W. Ingersoll photos, MHS
87. *Northwestern Builder and Decorator*, MHS
88. MHS
89. MHS
90. Kenneth M. Wright photo, MHS
91. MHS
92. MHS
93. MHS
95. MHS
97. *Independent Farmer and Fireside Companion*, MHS
98. MHS
99. MHS
100. Neil Currie photo, MHS
101. F. E. Haynes photo, MHS
102. MHS
104. MHS
105. MHS
106. Minnie and Martha Hoelzel photo, MHS
107. Carver County Historical Society
108. Carver County Historical Society
110. Ernest A. Hummel photo, MHS
111. MHS
112. MHS
114. Private collection
115. MHS
117. Oberholzer Foundation, MHS
118. *Detroit Lakes*, MHS
120. *Album of Views in and about Detroit Lakes*, MHS
121. E. D. Becker photo, MHS
123. MHS
124. Douglas County Historical Society
125*l*. Allen Latham
125*r*. C. L. Merryman photo, MHS
126. State Historic Preservation Office, Robert Frame photo, MHS
127. MHS
128. Marjorie Richison
129. Marjorie Richison; Marcia M. Sears and Joan M. Casari
130. MHS
131*l*. State Historic Preservation Office, Robert Frame photo, MHS
131*r*. State Historic Preservation Office, Robert Frame photo, MHS
132 State Historic Preservation Office, Robert Frame photo, MHS
133. Phil Hutchens photos, MHS
134. MHS
136. MHS
137. *Sheshebe Point, Lake Minnewawa*, MHS
138*l*. Itasca County Historical Society
138*r*. Nadine Martin Scrapbook, Itasca County Historical Society
139. Mark Haidet photo, MHS
140. Peel and Norton photo, MHS
142. Voyageurs National Park
143. Voyageurs National Park
144. Paul Larson photo
145. Paul Larson photo
146. Paul Larson photos
147. John Jager collection, Northwest Architectural Archives
148. State Historic Preservation Office, Liz Holum photo, MHS
149. Edwin Lundie collection, Northwest Architectural Archives

ESIGNED BY LOIS STANFIELD

LIGHTSOURCE IMAGES

TYPEFACE IS PALATINO

ARCHIVAL BLACK AND WHITE PHOTOGRAPHS

COLORED BY DESIGNER

USING DIGITAL IMAGING SOFTWARE